Pamela Des Barres

Biography

The Life Behind Music and the Love for Rock

CHRISTOPHER LEE WARD

The contents of this book may not be copied, reproduced or transmitted without the express written permission of the author or publisher. Under no circumstances will the publisher or author be responsible or liable for any damages, compensation or monetary loss arising from the information contained in this book, whether directly or indirectly. .

Disclaimer Notice:

Although the author and publisher have made every effort to ensure the accuracy and completeness of the content, they do not, however, make any representations or warranties as to the accuracy, completeness, or reliability of the content. , suitability or availability of the information, products, services or related graphics contained in the book for any purpose. Readers are solely responsible for their use of the information contained in this book

Every effort has been made to make this book possible. If any omission or error has occurred unintentionally, the author and publisher will be happy to acknowledge it in upcoming versions.

Copyright © 2024

All rights reserved

Table of Content

Chapter 1: Miss Japan Beautiful and the King

Chapter 2: The Happiest Broken Heart

Chapter 3: Love at First Sight

Chapter 4: Kicks

Chapter 5: Love in Her Eyes and Flowers in Her Hair

Chapter 6: The Virgin Groupie

Chapter 7: Absolute Beginners

Chapter 8: There's Only One Way to Rock

Chapter 9: Crazy, Crazy Nights

Chapter 10: Slow Dazzle

Chapter 11: Flesh for Fantasy

Chapter 12: A Chat Regarding the Infamous G Word

Chapter 13: Come as You Are

Chapter 14: The Male Groupie

Chapter 15: Miss You in a Heartbeat

Chapter 16: In So Deep

Chapter 17: Size Queen of the Stars

Chapter 1: Miss Japan Beautiful and the King

When I was barely old enough to tell the difference between the sexes, I dreamed of Elvis. His immaculate greasy quiff, smokey cheekbones, and rebellious insouciance epitomised a generation's yearning, making a certain slim, preteen Valley girl ecstatic. Years before puberty seized me between the legs, Elvis' undeniable carnal purity sent shivers down my spine. The unsullied depravity of his cry awoke lurking, tamed wantonness and produced a slippery peephole in spotless '50s squaredom all over the world. He loosened the screws on the earth's axis and then oiled it thoroughly with pomade.

And how he danced! Who knew human hips could move like that? I have an old-fashioned flip book showing Elvis whirling across the stage in his gold jacket, his knees at unusual angles, his pelvis thrusting forward, arms outstretched, eyes half-closed, sweat dripping with danger. Was it natural for the country lad truck driver to move that way? I'd always imagined Elvis was born with a completely new rhythm. But that was before I met the amazing Tura Satana, the doll who taught Elvis to dance both onstage and between the sheets.

When Elvis rose to popularity in the 1950s, the media kept its collective nose out of celebrity bedrooms, leaving us to speculate about what the King got up to under the covers. Years later, when word spread that he enjoyed seeing two lovelies go at it in nothing but white cotton underwear, the titillation factor skyrocketed. Even at his polyester sideshow Vegas apex, Elvis continued to captivate the masses (and misses), and rumours circulated that he dallied with many a lucky showgirl.

I was having a lively talk with the incredibly large Kitten Natividad when I observed my ex, Michael, deep in conversation with Tura. He drew my attention, giving me a look like, "Get your ass over here NOW!" Michael introduced us, stating that Tura had previously held the title of "Miss Japan Beautiful" and had been selected "one of America's Ten Best Undressed" with burlesque luminaries Lili St. Cyr and Tempest Storm. How couldn't I be impressed? I estimated that the lady was in her mid-sixties, and her cheeky, free-spirited demeanour immediately inspired me. She was slightly more zaftig than in her Kill days, but she wore her weight beautifully, dressed in a low-cut black costume with shining hair down to her ass. Loads of black eyeliner and glossy icy lips.

"There's something else you should know about the lovely Ms. Satana," Michael remarked with a twinkle in his baby blues, but Allee had just invited us to join the fun at the yum-laden buffet table. Several Beyond Dolls were excitedly comparing notes on the sizes of various actors' bodies. A showbiz wingding was described, in which three Hollywood stars unzipped and placed their products on a table for measurement. Because I had heard that one of the evening's competitors, Milton Berle, was gifted in that area, I was startled to learn that a particular A-list film actor emerged victorious that night. The Dolls started their own tournament, yelling out the names of the lucky dogs who shared their various boudoirs. I got into the spirit of things and shouted out a few of my own relevant headlines. But as Tura softly licked her lips and growled "Elvis Presley," everyone at the table knew they'd been licked too. I peered up through the velvety Valley smog and whispered a silent thank you to Jesus.

After supper, Siouxzan brings us to a pleasant, quiet den where we lie down on pillows beneath a big Pussycat poster of Tura's terrifying self as the vampy Varla. We have a couple glasses of red wine by candlelight, and the talk flows with the merlot. Tura's narrative is astonishing, dolls, and I recommend that you have an open mind. Simply sit back and enjoy the radiance.

Things got tougher on Chicago's west side. Tura was barely ten years old when she was raped by a gang of five men, one of whom turned out to be the cousin of the cop who arrived as she crawled out of the alleyway. A judge was bribed, and Tura ended up in reform school "for luring those boys into raping me." "I was classified as a juvenile delinquent." Tura couldn't abide being touched by anyone, including her parents, after the rape. She took a firm posture, eventually leading a raucous lady group, and found herself fending off "slant-eye" comments with her fists and wit. "We patrolled the neighbourhood to keep that kind of thing from happening to anybody else" . Tura's resilient temperament resulted in an enigmatic edginess that became part of her charm. Despite these limitations, her deepest desire was to sing and dance.

Tura regales me with stories of her circus performer mother, who taught her how to hula to her favourite song. "The 'Hawaiian War Chant' was really fast; that's how I learned to do some of my shimmies and moves". Tura stands and wriggles her hips with impressive ease and poise. "Mom loved Hawaiian music, particularly the percussion and electric guitars. You're naturally drawn to it."

More wine is poured, and I inquire about what distinguishes her performance from others on the tour. "I made my audience participate in my routine by talking to them, playing with them, and making jokes with them. I asked, "OK, where are your hands right now?" Tura quickly became a hothouse mainstay on the burlesque scene across the country, implying that there was a lot of action going on under the tables. Although she was initially sceptical, she quickly warmed up to her new form of self-expression since "the men in the audience wanted to adore you".

Long before the icky catastrophe of crotch-in-the-face lap dancing, strippers left a lot to the imagination. Burlesque was a beautiful art form in the 1950s, and Tura's costumes were beautifully beaded, highly decorated Asian rhapsodies that brought a man's natural geisha-girl fantasies to the forefront. She delicately balanced ornate headdresses, stroked long Japanese swords, and carefully slipped out of her hand-painted kimonos. Her prop Buddha was in his velvet-lined case, and as she touched his uplifted palms, he burst into flames.

After a wild night of tassel twirling for agog sailors in Biloxi, Mississippi, Tura met a certain budding rock and roll singer. "I was a big draw that night," she remembers with pleasure. It often took the teenage girl hours to relax after dishing out damp dreams to lusty strangers. Early this morning, she was cooling off by walking along the sand outside the club. "I was relaxing on the beach when this attractive guy approached me, and I replied, 'Nice night, isn't it?' 'Yes it is, ma'am'. 'Ma'am?' I was only sixteen years old and had never been addressed as ma'am' before. I had been lying about my age; everyone assumed I was nineteen. He asked, 'What are you doing out here so late at night?' I told him I was trying to decompress, and he asked, 'You too?'" The young pair strolled carefully along the shore, then sat on the sand and talked until the sun rose. "He said he did a show up the road, but I had no idea who he was." "Once I looked into those eyes of his, aahhh..." Tura has always had a thing for blue eyes. "I looked at his eyes and thought, 'Oh God, this one's a keeper'" . Later, she realised she hadn't even asked his name.

Elvis may have been shaking up the world, but even in 1956, he had the Colonel's minders watching his every movement. He was obviously smitten and wanted to be alone with Tura. He managed to avoid his two scheming sidekicks and take her to breakfast at an all-night diner. "He had the aura, and you knew he was going someplace. "I was drawn to him primarily by his smile," Tura admits wistfully. "And that Southern drawl would make your knees melt." Back then, he seemed so down to earth and natural. He was magnetic, attracting ladies left and right. He had a natural attraction.

Elvis and the exotic dancer started meeting secretly whenever possible. Tura slipped into his shows and was pleasantly delighted to see how he had adapted her shakes and shimmies into his own. "It was exciting to see him perform the moves on stage, especially because I was the one who taught him how. Also, how to do it in the bedroom was much better." Tura insisted on keeping their affair a secret so that it did not jeopardise his rapidly rising profession. She also did not expect him to be faithful. "When we were dating I said, 'I know you're going to have women throwing themselves at you and you're not gonna be able to say no'" . He replied, "I will, if you stay with me." Tura understood better. "There were guys who could say no, and guys who couldn't, and Elvis had no idea how to say no. He was always concerned about hurting people's sentiments. This is why they took advantage of him, particularly the Colonel. They walked all over him because he was so generous. "He was a down-home country boy who loved his mother."

Elvis was growing more passionately skilled, but there was one crucial romantic pleasure he had yet to discover. "Four or five nights later I showed him how to give head" . Tura grinned. "He hadn't done it yet" . Apparently, other ladies had tried to entice Elvis in that manner, but that particular feminine aroma turned him off. "I had just made love to him in the shower, so I said, 'Wait a minute! I cleansed you thoroughly before putting you in my mouth because I have no idea who you have been with. And the same goes for me. "I will not make love to anyone until I know I am clean."

Tura appears to have taught Elvis one of life's best sensual arts. "When a man wants to give you pleasure, that's what makes the difference—'Honey, don't be too rough there; just nibble, and when you discover that little man, nudge him. Multiple times. But try to do it gently at first... then a bit harder... after you've got him nice and hard, then you start to suck...''

Tura had been lonely on the road for a long time. "Then Elvis came along and he filled up a big empty hole, so to speak" , she exclaims. " Literally, too! It was wonderful while we were together. We were both really private people. He didn't appreciate the commotion around who he was dating." She acknowledged that the studios forced Elvis to date his co-stars, but it hurt.

One night after Tura performed in Memphis, a devoted, obsessed admirer went into his car, loaded a double-barrel shotgun into his mouth, and discharged the trigger because she refused to date him. Elvis arrived in his pink Cadillac to pick up Tura and discovered the gruesome sight. The cops were harassing her, as if she had something to do with the unfortunate situation. "The shotgun was still in his mouth and his brains were on the backseat" , stated Tura, "and when Elvis got there he said, 'Baby, they ain't ever gonna put you through anything like this again'" . That night, he presented her with a diamond engagement ring and claimed her as his own. "It was completely unexpected—he turns around, grabs me, kisses me, and says, 'God, do you know how much I love you?' He reaches into his pocket and takes out a package containing this stunning diamond ring." Yes, I did notice the huge flashing diamond on Tura's finger. Swoon. Elvis' ring. "It's three and a half carats," she says, smiling. "I said, 'What is it for', and he said, 'I just asked you to marry me', and I responded, 'You did?' At first, I replied yes. I wasn't expecting that because he knew I had a minor altercation with the Colonel".

Tura wore the ring for a while, but Hollywood kept beckoning the King to the silver screen. Elvis informed her he didn't want to keep their engagement a secret any longer, but he was squirting actresses. Tura noticed the photographs in cinema publications. When she tried to return the ring, Elvis told her to keep it. "He refused to accept it, saying, 'That's part of me and you. You'll always belong to me as long as you wear that ring. I answered, 'No, I won't. I will no longer belong to you. From now on, I'll go out with other guys and do what I do best."

Elvis was still thinking about Tura Satana when he brought the teenage Priscilla Beaulieu home to Memphis from the army. "He always found my phone number no matter how many times I changed it", she relates. "We were friends, but he wanted to return to the physical side of our relationship. I have always said no." The imported sweet-faced brunette who would become Mrs. Presley gradually resembled a certain Asian burlesque siren. The hair grew darker and piled higher on her head, and her eyes, thick with black eyeliner, tilted dangerously upward. "He said he wanted a replica of me, and I said, 'She's a completely different person.'" He answered, 'But I can make her look like you'. I told him it wasn't fair to Priscilla, and he said, 'But I want you, and I can't have you'."

Oh, what a night! Slightly tipsy and reeling from all the heady Elvis revelations, I thank the gracious Ms. Satana and collect my belongings. We exchanged hugs and agreed to stay in touch. Before I go out into the leafy night, I ask Tura if she has ever wished things had been different. "I know Elvis was attempting to get off the meds he was taking", she recalls, "but he gained so much weight that he felt he had to go back on the pills. Nobody was caring for or feeding him properly. They simply allowed him to binge on his favourite dishes, deep-fried Southern fare that was bad for him." Tura feels unhappy and gently shakes her head. "When he died, I always believed that if I had been with him, I could have gotten him through. I would have influenced him more than the Colonel or anyone else." As Tura runs her hands through her long black hair, Elvis' diamond ring sparkles in the candlelight.

Chapter 2: The Happiest Broken Heart

Cherry vanilla. Her moniker evokes the flamboyant, blatant, shameless exuberance of her most adventurous decade, the gloriously unabashed 1970s. Look Cherry up on the Internet, and thousands of entries appear, all of which revere this punk high priestess.

While I was tearing up the Sunset Strip in my garters and leopard-print spike heels, I realised I had a terrific counterpart on the East Coast. In those days, groupie tom-toms were the most trustworthy source of information about who was doing what with whom behind closed hotel room doors. I knew Cherry was a member of Andy Warhol's impudent entourage, as well as a member of David Bowie's tight-knit inner circle who worked as his überpublicist for MainMan. She hung out with a number of great rockers and made a couple of filthy rock and roll albums of her own, Bad Girl and Venus D'Vinyl.

Before our scheduled rendezvous in Los Angeles, I played her two records. Five years ago, Bad Girl and Venus D'Vinyl were reissued as a double album, and I thoroughly enjoyed her nervy lyrics and noisy tongue-in-cheek humour.

Cherry has lived in the same classic deco two-story building on Hollywood Boulevard for two decades, and before we begin remembering, I go through her elegant apartment, admiring her varied art collection and marvelling at images of her carousing with the famous and infamous.

We snuggle into a nice corner on a vintage couch, and when I ask Cherry how she got started in music, I learn that both of us had a memorable early experience with a specific Italian crooner.

"My mother worked as a telephone operator at Hotel 14 in Manhattan, which housed the Copacabana. If I was a good little girl, my father would take me down the elevators and into the kitchen, the same way the stars entered the Copa. I watched Jimmy Durante, Eartha Kitt, and Tony Bennett, and I remember mink stoles draped over chair backs, the scent of perfume in the air, the dazzle of jewellery, and the clink of glasses. And the Copa choir girls with pastel-coloured hair! They might be dressed in pastel blue for Tony Bennett's act, with matching hair dye. Jimmy Durante's outfits and hair would be pale orange. "You can imagine how that stuck with me." I surely can, as Cherry's hair has changed colour each time I've seen her. In Fairmount, it was vibrant pink; now it's pastel turquoise. "Those are the little glimpses I remember," she sighs. "I have a tale that explains how I became a fan and groupie. In fact, my ambition to be involved in the entertainment business developed right there and then. Martin and Lewis were still together when I was eight or nine in '51 or '52. I'd watched them on TV and liked their performance. Back then, the hotel employed the same staff year after year. So, when the stars returned, they became pals, like a small family. My mother introduced me to all of the bellhops, and they decided to play a prank on Dean Martin. He came in every night at six p.m. to change for the super performance, so one of the bellhops took me up to his room and set me on the side of his bed. I was there by myself, waiting for Dean Martin. I was already in love with him; he was so attractive. The adrenaline! So I was sitting there arranging my tiny dress when he stepped in, the most handsome thing I'd ever seen—bigger, darker, shinier, taller, softer, sweeter—everything I'd hoped for. I recall everything he wore: brown wool slacks, a brown and white wool tweed jacket, a bright white shirt, a brown tie, and black shining hair. He said, 'Oh, hi! Who are you? I said, 'I'm Mary's daughter, Kathleen. He said, 'Well, great to meet you'. I can't recall what we talked about, but Dean Martin and I did! Then he added, 'I have to go do my program now, so I'll contact your mother and tell her to come fetch you.'"

I can empathise because when I was thirteen, I wore my frothiest junior high pre-prom dress and was invited to be in the audience for Dean Martin's TV show. I was fortunate that my exotic uncle Hamil choreographed the hit series, teaching Dino's perfectly coiffed, Day-Glo-clad Gold Diggers their daring moves. I was the ideal age to sigh and drool over Dean's beautiful carefree attitude, and I stared at my autographed eight-by-ten until his ballpoint signature faded.

In 1961, Cherry began working at an advertising agency while also attending night school to learn film production and acting. "It was the early 1960s when the Peppermint Lounge opened and discos began," Cherry exclaims eagerly. "The first discotheque I visited was Le Club on East 55th Street. The music began softly during dinner, then became louder and more dance-y as the night progressed. It was a revelation because I was eighteen and ready for it. Following Le Club, there was Le Introde. I worked at an ad agency during the day and DJed at Aux Puces on weekends. I was influenced by many different musical genres, but my favourite was rock & roll. It was incredible—you suddenly had the Peppermint Lounge, with Jackie Kennedy and Lee Radziwill swaying and performing the Twist, but also 42nd Street hookers. It was the first time you witnessed this clash of cultures, which is what made discos like Aux Puces and Arthur so fascinating. People of all financial levels, social classes, and vocations found themselves dancing together in the same location. That was the greatest miracle of all. I thought, 'Wow, the world is finally accepting this. Rock and roll is here to stay. Then came Flower Power, which we expected to be even more stunning."Cherry was still known as Kathleen Dorritie at the time, but she had started using clever aliases like Indian Summer and Party Favour. "During the Vietnam War, I met Richard Skidmore, who worked for the left-wing militant Abbie Hoffman. They made tapes that were smuggled into Radio Hanoi, which were essentially black radical propaganda. I knew I wanted the war to stop, but I lacked political knowledge. They instructed me to record a tape like a DJ, playing my favourite songs and telling hot anecdotes to entertain the troops. I thought I was doing a great job by telling them how I screwed this and that one. I could see a soldier in the field jerking off to it. Years later, I questioned, oh my God, what were they actually using me for? So we were in this improvised studio when Richard said, 'You shouldn't use your own name because the government doesn't like these tapes. I think I saw the name on an ice cream container, but I can't remember. So I said, "Okay, how about cherry vanilla?" I hadn't intended for it to continue, but I finally began writing for Circus and Creem. The first few pieces were published under my name, but then they asked, 'Why don't you use Cherry Vanilla?

Cherry went to work the next day, but she couldn't concentrate, so she left early and hitchhiked to Jersey just as the curtain rose on Guess Who. But, guess what happened. "I was really delighted to spend another night with Burton. Backstage, however, he seemed detached. The band repeatedly said, 'Come with us to Virginia Beach!' So I boarded the bus. Burton had nothing to do with me, even though I didn't even have an overnight bag. The boys said, 'Oh, you know how Burton is', because I was plainly done. "He had cooled on me." But Cherry persevered, crashing platonically with band members and wearing the same dress for three days. "They dumped me off in the Bronx, and I had to ride the train in this filthy clothes. I felt that everyone was looking at me, that I was ashamed, and that Burton no longer loved me. But I penned a poem titled 'A Groupie Lament'. I didn't consider myself a groupie, even though I enjoyed musicians, until I saw the film Groupies, starring Cynthia Plaster Caster. You were also involved. When I saw that, I thought, "Yeah!" It's okay to call oneself a groupie. I am a groupie! "Call me a groupie!" And fuck everything, at least I got a poem out of it!"

Some musicians had more of an impact than others. "When I met Kris Kristofferson, he was only a small folkie playing coffee shops in the Village. He was fantastic, one of the most romantic, a very loving man, and excellent in bed. This is a weird story: I saw images of him and heard him sing and thought, 'I have to have sex with this man'. So I waited in line for the first show at the Gaslight Cafe. It was a little coffee shop with benches seating 60 or 70 people, and I had to sit at the back. When everyone cleared out, I went to the ladies' room, waited until the second act, and took a seat directly in front of the stage. I was by myself the entire time, staring at him and virtually touching him. I penned a four-line poem and handed it to him as he exited the stage. As everyone stood up to leave, he peeked out of the dressing room and remarked, 'OK, you got me'. Isn't it cute? 'You got me'. So I went backstage to hang out with him."

Cherry's generosity in sharing her reward struck me as admirable. "Oh certainly," she smiles, "we used to offer our best to one other. And someone else was coming next week: Leon Russell! So, who cared? I first met Leon at the Capitol Theatre during the Mad Dogs and Englishmen tour. That was the ultimate run-away-with-the-circus trip for me, when I believed I could get on the bus and never return to reality. The music was incredible, and the environment was inviting, family-oriented, and constant fun. I developed an instant connection with the Okies in the band, particularly Chuckie Blackwell, the gorgeous golden boy drummer. He was a tiny devil and a true sex maniac who could fuck and fuck for hours on end. And playful, possibly bisexual, with a million laughs in between orgasms. I genuinely loved him, not as a girlfriend, but as a true sex companion. Through Chuckie, I gradually got to know Leon—as much as anyone can. He's a quiet, keep-to himself type of man. Of course, I was madly in love with his music and wanted to get as close to him as possible, which for me at the moment meant sleeping with him. Chuckie and Leon were sharing a room with twin beds. I had sex with Chuckie, followed by sex with Leon. I can't say that was the most exciting sex I've ever had, especially not with Chuckie. Chuckie Blackwell was unlike anyone else in rock and roll when it came to sex. But I got to be close to Leon for a few hours and give him the gift of my love in exchange for all the pleasure his music had brought me."I'm full of inquiries regarding the mysterious Mr. Warhol. Was he mysterious? Amusing? Quiet? "He was childish towards me. He'd whisper in my ear during a gathering, "I hear that boy has a big penis." Why don't you go see it, then come back and tell me about it? He was inquisitive, cute, and eager to hear stories. He would boost your ego by stating, "You are so fabulous." "If only Hollywood knew who the true stars are, it would be a different world." Others had issues with him. I believe they came to rely on him for money, but I never did. This was an equity play, so we received a salary and did not expect Andy to pay our rent. When I auditioned for him, I realised that he enjoyed advertising. I had done an ad for Yodora deodorant for black people, which would be extremely racist nowadays. But we used to claim it was designed for Negro skins. He just ate it up! He was also interested in Catholicism, so he inquired into Catholic schools.

A woman's ability to build a name for herself in the music industry was far more difficult in 1970. "I wanted to be necessary, so I figured, 'Wow, I'm getting in there. I actually am in show business. Oh, that was the most magical summer! The cast lived together. Rod Stewart and his band, America, visited our apartment. Many local musicians would sleep in our flat. We had a blast. Andy visited for a few days before we opened. And we had a wonderful opening night party."

Cherry continues her intrepid story: "We were in Boston one night, Angie was not present, and I ended up in bed with Bowie. And, oh, did I want that from the moment I met him! They had an "open marriage," but I had never had the opportunity till then. I also worked for him, and Angie was both his wife and my friend. So, even though I was this crazy animal, it felt strange. If I were going to do it, I was going to sneak! It was fantastic. Bowie makes an excellent lover because he, too, is romantic. Although it is possible to get the impression that he is acting, who cares? Bowie is an actor. That's how I feel in life as well. Whatever job you acquire, you wear the uniform and costume and act as if you were in a play. Romance improved lovemaking, although I didn't always pursue it. I went home with guys I knew were into S&M and did some strange things because I wanted to try it all. The missionary position for a guy and a woman is ideal because you can kiss while coming. Who does not adore it? Bowie was really good, athletic, strong, and entertaining. Tony DeFries, however, forbade being with David. Members of the staff were not supposed to do that. We'd been in Tony's room earlier, and Bowie made me sit in the same chair as him. DeFries was insisting, 'You better have those contracts typed by tomorrow'. It was all the more fascinating since it was forbidden. There were drugs on the tour, but we did them nonetheless. But by the time I started working for Bowie, I had little time for sex with anyone else. Girls, including Angie Bowie, did not appeal to me. There were a few groupies on the road, but by the time I worked for him in '72, '73, and '74, my major groupie days were done. They kind of ended with Bowie.

Cherry has spent the previous eight years collaborating with Vangelis, a world-renowned Greek composer/artist well known for his beautiful Chariots of Fire soundtrack. "I met him at the RCA offices while we were both on RCA. He's the same age as me: sixty-two. He was unlike anyone I had ever been with before. I've always adored thin, small rock and roll boys. I fell in love with a man of my age who was both intelligent and nice. I fell in love in an entirely different way. Vangelis began sending me requests to make minor 'speak' things on his songs, using whatever reason he could find. Then one time, I ended up having sex with him. We had sex a few more times before wondering what to do next. Am I meant to be your girlfriend? But we both knew we wouldn't be boyfriend and girlfriend since I was just too independent. So we thought, "What are we going to do?" We love each other, but we know it won't work. He stated, "We will love each other and be friends forever." He was correct; we are. So here I am, working for him. "And look!" Cherry grins, putting out her arm, "He gave me a $15,000 watch for my sixtieth birthday!"

Chapter 3: Love at First Sight

In August 1966, Enny Bruce, the poster punk for fearless rulebreakers, died of heroin addiction, which had been compounded by a lot of court-appointed ballbusting. When I was almost seventeen, I dressed in Grandma's velvet and went to Lenny's final resting place to pay my respects. After joining the colourful crowd walking around the cemetery, I ended up at a tragically cool eulogy hosted in a hipster's backyard in Woodland Hills. I sat cross-legged on the ground, beside several sombre-faced groovers, as Lenny's peers paid him an angry tribute. I paid close attention to Phil Spector, who stated that Lenny had died "from an overdose of police". I attempted to concentrate on the proceedings, but brightly coloured splotches from another part of the yard kept drawing my attention.

A few months after Lenny's eulogy, I rested my Twiggified eyes on Frank Zappa again. My childhood best friend Iva Turner and I were among the hippies and freaks protesting the closure of our favourite club, Pandora's Box, on Sunset and Crescent Heights. Immediate danger hung in the air, but just as a hundred baton-wielding cops marched toward us, I spotted Frank Zappa among the colourful crowd. I instinctively caressed his wild hair, then looked at Iva and amazed, "It's soft...". My second Zappa sighting was at the Cheetah Club, where I rolled around on the floor with Frank before being formally presented to the wonderful rock icon.

We arrived at the infamous log cabin in Laurel Canyon, long owned by 1920s Hollywood cowboy Tom Mix, all decked out to impress the maestro. His adored four-legged co-star, Tony the Wonder Horse, was said to be buried beneath the basement bowling alley. Upstairs, there was a fireplace the size of a movie star's wardrobe, and Frank sat nearby at his piano, creating cryptic masterpieces.

Between our countless pressing commitments, Gail and I find time to have multiple cups of tea in her overcrowded kitchen. Gail has remodelled, but I remember exactly where the intercom was when I was a governess: when four-year-old Moon's sweet voice would wake me up, asking me to come in and make "breaktess" while Keith Moon waited impatiently in my little guest house, wearing my leopard print spiked heels.

After we eat loads of spicy Indian food, Gail and I discuss a variety of issues while the family dogs snurfle for attention and the cats wander lazily across the tablecloth. Even after decades of late-night chats with Gail, I learn a lot more about her during the next several hours.

Gail's nuclear scientist father, Jack, was a captain in the United States Navy, and the Sloatmans relocated frequently as she grew up. He led the Office of Naval Research in London, and while there in the mid-1960s, teenage Gail discovered deep new possibilities when she went to a party for an up-and-coming rock band.

Since I've known Gail, she's had an eerily predictive sense of the future, which appears to have surfaced early on. "I had psychic visions on an oddly consistent basis", she acknowledges. "When I was just eighteen years old, I obtained my first job in London working for the American Embassy since my family had diplomatic passports. And I'll tell you this: on March 16, 1964, while working, this prophetic poetry came to me out of nowhere. So I had to type it up, and I remember the date because it was my father's birthday. I realised from this piece of poetry that I was somewhat protected. All I had to do was wait, and this essential person would arrive. I knew he was out there and would show up. I didn't pursue any specific interests because I knew I'd meet this guy, and my entire life would be unthinkable compared to what it was then." Did she develop genuine feelings for anyone while hurling herself around London? "I had a 'crunch' on Chris Stamp, one of The Who's managers. It wasn't something serious—there was a lot of sex for enjoyment back then."

Gail met her first serious lover, Terence Donovan, a British fashion photographer, on a modelling shoot. "He was the third person I slept with, and he completely seduced me —it was fabulous' ' . She continued to see Terence even after moving to New York at the age of nineteen, when she became acquainted with the legendary groupie/backup vocalist Emmaretta Marks.

"This is what happens when you don't want to be the groupie you always wanted to be. Oh, how many groupies would have been envious of my circumstance, when all I wanted was escape. I was at a record company party for Tom Jones with Emeretta at the Carlyle, but it got later and later, and eventually the trains stopped operating to Long Island, and she vanished on me. It's suddenly down to the last few individuals, and I don't have a ride or a place to stay, so I'm not sure what the fuck I'm going to do. Tom apparently thinks I am a little morsel and offers, 'How would you like to spend the night with me?' I thought, 'Well, I wouldn't! 'How will I get out of this?' It was the normal silent conversation you have with yourself: you're in a guy's room, and they really do expect it; they believe you're there on purpose, with your intention. I was very uninterested in him because he embodied everything I disliked about the pop world—he was completely commercial, serious about taking himself seriously, and I couldn't understand what his thousands of admirers saw in him. Anyway, I was stranded in this hotel room thinking, 'What the heck am I gonna do?'"

Gail ran to the bathroom with the bright notion of stuffing towels down the toilet, forcing a plumber to be called. "The most exciting news of all was the bathroom telephone. I contacted my mother and told her I was desperate, stranded in a hotel room, and wanted her to know I was safe, and she answered, 'Well, you ought to be ashamed of yourself, and by the way, Lou called and he's looking for you'". Another of Gail's groovy boyfriends was music producer Lou Adler, who salvaged the night after receiving a call from her mother by sending a car to the Carlyle, whisking the mortified young damsel away from impending disaster. "He saved my rock and roll ass", she laughs.And how did Tom react to her skedaddling? "He was a gentleman, and absolutely charming about it, but he was agitated" .

She was only in New York for six months, yet she managed to cheer up a young blues musician. "In 1965, New York was filled with Jewish men playing the blues. Emeretta performed with The Blues Project. One day, their leader, Al Kooper, declared that I was his lover. He took this decision without telling me; I did not have a sexual relationship with Mr. Cooper. I've heard that in his autobiography, he writes something about sending me screaming into Frank Zappa's arms, which is false.

Gail's description of her neighbourhood coffee business reveals that she enjoys reminiscing. "If you enter Book Soup right now, you'll notice a closed door at an angle to the main store. The door was constantly open, and there was a stairwell leading up to our apartment. Find that door, imagine there's a table next to it, and imagine Jim Morrison sitting there every day. The Doors were the house band at the Whisky, and I met him there for coffee virtually every day. However, this was not planned. I glanced at him, and he looked at me, and he asked that I sit down, and we had this chat, 'You feel so familiar, look so familiar, I feel like I know you.'" How did she reject the evident allure of the Lizard King? "Let's just say he had a fascinating relationship with every girl that crossed my path, but not with me. Later, we discovered that we had known each other since we were five years old. "His father was also in the navy."

When Gail's supervisor at the Trip, Elmer Valentine, hired her to work at his other Strip venue, the Whisky a Go Go, she resisted his advances as well. "I had always heard that he was a lecher, but not in a negative sense. What is the definition of a lecher? The Whisky was like a large candy store; who wouldn't want to indulge in the goodies? I believe Mario and Elmer provided the best protection and knowledge for any young girl in Hollywood. They were quite kind and looked out for you."

Gail had a similar encounter with the universe about this time. "I decided to take acid to see what everyone was talking about. It wasn't banned; people continued to put it on sugar cubes and store it on trays in the refrigerator. So I took acid. When I tried to create a face, the eyelashes kept moving, then stopped moving. It was interesting because I came to terms, in some tiny way, with what I thought I knew about thinking. Whoa. I asked Gail to allow me to take a deep breath and sip tea to process my thoughts.I had to take it again to see whether that was a real evaluation, and I came to the conclusion that if you think you're going to have a paranoid experience, you probably will. I believe acid did the reverse of what everyone believed, by extending your consciousness. Instead, it enables you to narrow your attention in a targeted and polished manner. Everything is contained within one item, no matter how little. It's a map of the whole cosmos. It was as deep as you let yourself go. In that sense, it felt like you were expanding your consciousness simply by looking at something closely and observing it in a way you hadn't previously. The difficulty was that you had no control over it, and when under the influence, your response was restricted by time and a loss of intensity. But I felt like I was getting the gist of the story. There were no rules since you were taking big risks, but you were so young that you didn't consider them risks. Someone has been telling you for a long time that you can't do this and shouldn't do that or bad things will happen. You suddenly realised that there had never been anyone else. It was always up to you to believe what was offered to you. So I said, "Fuck that; I'll never have to listen to anyone again."

An unusual girl who worked with Gail at the Whisky surprised her one afternoon. "She was one of those girls with long, straight hair, continually tossing it about in her hands and huffing and puffing whenever she passed by. I never thought she liked me since she was constantly scrutinising me. One day, she started gazing at me, so I thought, 'Well, I can play this game' and gazed back. I knew it would be about who blinked first—it was that stupid—so instead of blinking, she said, 'Okay, I'd like you to come over to my house for dinner,' which broke the ice with her. When Gail walked into the house on Kirkwood and smelled sizzling lamb chops, she recalled she had been there recently. The grumpy girl was Pamela Zarubica, the voice of Suzy Creamcheese, and her roommate was Frank Zappa. "We hadn't even finished supper when the phone rang—it was Frank. He requested to be picked up from the airport because his promotional tour had been cut short. Pamela stated, 'He warned me not to bring anyone, but we're heading to the airport. I recall thinking she was trying to hook us up. So I proceeded to the airport, and the rest was history."

Were they both aware that this was it? "Well, we got back to the house, and he didn't say anything except about the tour. Pamela once stated, 'I'm going to sleep in your bed so you guys can take mine. Frank had a single bed, whereas she had a double. Then she offered me a small black slip to wear. Frank was exhausted from travelling, so we climbed into bed and hugged, but nothing occurred. "He was a perfect gentleman."

Was she concerned that her fait accompli would land her in trouble? "Yeah, I felt nervous, but it is possible to be both nervous and comfortable. The next morning, I woke up, returned to my body, realised where I was, and thought, 'Oh God, I think he's awake'. I rolled over, and the cushion was like a mountain. All I could see was one eye, wide open, over the edge of the cushion, staring at me. I heard my voice say, "OK, this is it, and if you don't accept it, you won't hear from us again."

Was Mr. Zappa aware he had met his cosmic match? "I never knew that—I didn't know for years, until I read an interview in which he said that when he met me, it was love at first sight." It's such a cheesy thing to say—something you wouldn't expect him to say, but he had a way with clichés."

& how did this nascent rock & roll relationship develop? "I knew Frank was the one that morning, but nothing changed. Then he called and asked me out on a certain day three days later. Following the Lenny Bruce eulogy, we had a gig. I recall stopping at the Whisky to get Frank's amplifier. I was trying to drag this massive item out the front door, and Mario wasn't helping. He grabbed my shirt and exclaimed, 'You're not wearing a bra!' "

After living with the Zappas on and off for a few years, I believe that much of the enchantment I experienced between Frank and Gail sprang from her sparing him from excursions to Ralphs and other trivialities of life. "Oh yeah," she agrees. "Bad things could happen at Ralphs" . I inform her that this chapter may be seen as a guidebook for aspiring groupies. "Whenever I've had to answer inquiries in forms such, 'What is your profession?' I would always write 'professional wife'. I never, ever put 'housewife' or 'wife' on a form because it is a fucking job that can be done properly or poorly."

I believe that certain brilliant artists, such as Picasso, Shakespeare, or Mozart, were most likely not ordinary people and thus could not be expected to function at their peak when dealing with basic day-to-day tasks. Gail laughs, "It was really more about if he didn't get to do what he wanted, awful things would happen. I simply never stood in the way. I had witnessed his dissatisfaction with the business side of things and told myself, 'Don't believe you're going to help him in business. He'll make his own decisions, and nothing you say will change that. Another thing I recognized was that I did not want to be a part of the problem that prevents him from completing his task.

I remind Gail that I have always thought of her as astutely intelligent as her wonderful husband was in her own way. "I can't drink that," she says, laughing. "There's curds and there's whey, you know what I'm saying?".

Something incomprehensible between Frank and Gail clearly worked. There were moments when I had to cover my head with pillows to get some sleep as they worked. Deep down, I wished I could have such a pleasantly raucous sex life. "Really?". Gail says, slightly surprised, "I'm very sorry. I had no idea. That's the thing: sex doesn't change; it only gets better."

Was there a time when she considered leaving Frank? "I never considered leaving him for another woman, but I did consider leaving him because it became too much at times. When we were at the log cabin, I left." What?? I'm stunned. Did she genuinely flee their lovely Laurel Canyon sanctuary? "Yeah, I just said, 'I've had it,' and walked out one day. I scrawled Frank a letter in lipstick on the upstairs bathroom mirror so only he could see it, then took the baby and boarded the plane. We had become a crash pad! Anyone may dwell there at any moment; there were no locks on any doors, and Moon and I were not given precedence. It felt hazardous for both me and my munchkin. What you didn't realise was that I had no means of transportation and had to hitchhike to do the laundry. I had to stick my thumb out on Laurel Canyon Boulevard to get to the freakin grocery store. There was not even a proper floor in the kitchen. Nobody had the time. And then they'd ask, 'How come there's no food in the house? Well, I don't know; why don't you ask Mercy?"

I was never ashamed to be a groupie. I relish and revel in the gorgeous, twangy odes that my songwriting partner, Mike Stinson, composes for me, and I still consider myself a muses.

I tell Gail that I feel Bob Dylan, my all-time hero, marked the much-needed shift in consciousness. "Well, I didn't think of Dylan as hardcore rock and roll, but I did recognize that he was transforming my perception of the art form. I was familiar with the origins of the songs that he and others in the New York folk culture sang and wrote about. Some were really engaged in history, while others performed pop music. Peter, Paul, and Mary were all singing traditional folk music, but Dylan stood out. What he was writing was entirely congruent with the massive shift in consciousness. In that respect, he was just as rock and roll as everyone else. When I first arrived in

Hollywood, I attended a large party in the hills. There were large, open doors that went out onto a spacious balcony. I stepped outside to look around, and there was no one there. I was alone at this balustrade, and it was a stunningly lovely night. I was in California and thought, 'This is amazing'. As I turned to go to the door, this guy appeared around the corner. I knew it was Bob Dylan. I thought he was gorgeous. He was really stunning, as were all of us at the time. The question was, 'Do I just stop in my tracks and let him pass?' because, well, it's Bob Dylan. But I kept walking, and as we glanced at each other, he said, 'Hello'. I can't even express this idyllic Southern California evening—there you are, and there he is. "Bob Dylan greets you, and then you walk on..."

Chapter 4: Kicks

I've been attracted by Cynthia Plaster Caster's bold art since 1968, when my artistic mentor, Frank Zappa, first told me about her. I'm a huge fan of rock stars myself, and I was amazed by the clever method she went about meeting her personal favourites. Frank saw Cynthia as an inventive trailblazer and decided that the shy, pudgy, dark-haired girl from Chicago should join his zany ranks, even if her particular art style couldn't be recorded on vinyl. Fortunately, our squealy first meeting was preserved when Frank introduced us over the phone and recorded our giggly call for a tune on Permanent Damage, my all-girl group's album.

I'm always delighted when our busy schedules allow for a quick visit, so when Cynthia called to inform me that one of her favourite new bands, the Redwalls, had asked her to appear in their next video here in Los Angeles, I jumped for excitement. Of course, I offered her to stay with me, and in between our noisy dinner party and shopping trips, Cynthia and I were able to curl up on the couch and trip the light fantastic.

Cynthia, like myself, was struck hard by the lime-coloured lightning bolt known as the Beatles. Until then, she had been a fan of show tunes and live theatre, so when she saw a photo of the four mop tops in identical attire, she assumed they were a new comedy team. "Then I heard 'I Wanna Hold Your Hand' and was blown away —because they were good looking and made proportionately great music". Cynthia, while being virginal and entirely uninformed of life's reality, recognized that there were many more exciting options to contemplate. "Fuck the high school swillers. "This is what I want to date!"

Cynthia arrived with her best friend, Pest, to find three girls waiting at the hotel; the next day, there were six. Cynthia excitedly handed Brian Jones a package of cough drops and collected Mick and Keith's autographs, but she realised there had to be a better way to meet the band.

Until she briefly met Gene Clark of the Byrds, Cynthia thought all she wanted was to make out with her musical heroes. "We spoke with Gene, and he replied, 'Oh, you're virgins, huh? Why?' 'Why shouldn't we be virgins?' "Because sex feels good!" What, Gene? 'You are kidding!' Pest didn't believe it either, so we wondered, 'How does it feel good?' I mean, nobody in high school mentioned it."

The Hollies were the first British group with whom the girls had the opportunity to spend significant time. "They were the first band I ever hung out with one-on-one. But not the cute ones; it was Bobby Elliott, the drummer, and Eric Haydock, the teddy-bear bassist. We managed to go into their hotel room and joked with them; we enjoyed British humour. And because they weren't the band's main rock stars, we felt more like equals.

Their semi-comfortable experience must have prompted "I want more of this!"

Clever, clever, clever. Cynthia and Pest were on their way to a possible pop heaven as the competition became fierce and girls piled up in the lobbies. They started leaving filthy letters for the musicians. "We used Cockney rhyming terminology in these ridiculous notes, such as 'Hello, Gerry and the Pacemakers. We are the Barclay's Bankers in Chicago. We offer convenient midnight hours. "Do you want to make a deposit?"

The Dick Clark Caravan of Stars visited Chicago in April 1966, and Paul Revere and the Raiders headlined this trip. "Their song 'Kicks' reached number one on the charts, which was extremely popular! Because, as you know, one of the appeals of being a groupie is impressing your peers with the band's fame and success—especially when we were younger. Not only were the men attractive and accomplished, but it was also a delightful experience.I was an art major who was on my way out of class to meet Pest and locate the motel. We had no idea how we were going to meet them, but we assumed we'd use the 'passing the note' approach. I stopped dead in my tracks when my art teacher gave us the homework assignment: 'Make a plaster cast', he said, and the thing had to be substantial. 'Solid! I thought, "Wait a moment." 'Doesn't Hampton Wicks get solid? Okay, let's make it extremely ludicrous. I took additional plaster and put it in a brown paper bag labelled PLASTER to make it look professional. I couldn't wait to tell Pest, and she had the same reaction as I did—we both yelled! We carried the kit to the hotel and located Paul Revere and the Raiders' rooms."

Cynthia had never seen a penis before and had no idea how to handle one when she and Pest knocked on the first hotel room door. The Raiders were excellent sports, assuring the girls they'd come up with a brilliant idea and leading them to the next room till they reached the vocalist, Mark Lindsay.

Cynthia submitted a plaster vegetable as an assignment, but her ambitions were far greater. "After that weekend, Pest and I were Chicago's Plaster Casters. It was so stupid, yet that was all we wanted to be! I put a generic-looking logo on the side of a little case and thought, 'We should really learn how to do this, put all the stuff in the luggage, and make ourselves look like salesmen, moving from hotel to hotel'. The bands thought it was hilarious, and the word spread quickly—long before we figured out how to actually produce a cast!"

As "The Last Train to Clarksville" climbed the pop charts, teenybop fans assumed the Monkees were as innocent as their catchy songs, but groupies knew different. The mod TV quartet passed through Chicago, and as Cynthia and Pest waited outside the hotel, a couple of roadies welcomed them up. "We were out there with a large number of girls and were singled out because of that fucking suitcase".

The Plaster Casters of Chicago quickly found themselves in front of a willing Monkee. "I attempted to open the can, which opened up like Planter's Peanuts in those days, and it's dangerous because you may seriously cut yourself. Which I did, and my pinkie finger wouldn't stop bleeding." Cynthia felt compelled to apologise as Peter Tork stood ready, able, and naked. "That got me off the hook, thank goodness, because I later discovered you have to be more scientific with alginates." The water cannot be excessively hot or chilly. The ideal approach to mix is with your hands, carefully, without creating too many air bubbles, and keeping an eye on the water temperature."

As she contemplated these fundamental creative topics, difficulties arose at home. "All this time, the Warden had been reading my journals, each and every one. So Mom discovered I was no longer a virgin and grounded me for a month.

Cynthia had to leave college and find work, despite the fact that she was doing well. "It was scary. I didn't know what the Warden would do to me if I fell asleep. She was sneaky, trying to influence me behind my back by tossing out Beatles memorabilia—she threw away my Beatles dolls!" How dare she! The nerve! What injustice! Cynthia had gained forty pounds as a result of the Wardens punishment, and it came at the worst possible time.

"We had our heyday for approximately two or three years, and I was overweight the entire time. It was really difficult to lose that weight once I fled from the Warden. I had one more small scene with Mark Lindsay, but I had gained weight and I believe he was no longer interested in my figure. In fact, the next time he came into town, he was with another girl, and I was devastated."

The Experience was doing two concerts at the Civic Opera House, and after the first, Cynthia, Dianne, and Marilyn, another die-hard rock fan, followed Hendrix to the Hilton Hotel. "When we showed them the luggage with our brand on the side, they began waving and following us. We couldn't believe it—they were the most popular band at the moment. Noel introduced a new style of looking groovy in Britain: large Afro-curly hair and psychedelic clothes, this impish little boy; nothing was more English than the elfin appearance. When we arrived at the hotel, they looked at us, and we looked at them—in person! And Jimi responds, 'Ohhhh yes, I've heard about you from someone in the Cosmos—come on up to my hotel room. The first huge excitement was travelling in the elevator with the band, rather than charging up the fire escape. There were six of us in this small elevator: Jimi, Noel, Mitch, Dianne, and Marilyn. And we didn't say anything".

All these years later, I'm still astounded that Hendrix handled this novel event with such ease, as if having his penis plastered for posterity was routine. "Yeah, he was perfectly comfortable," Cynthia says. "Dianne gives him a blow job, and he has this very enormous, honkin' — it's true what they say about black men. So he dipped his dick in the alginates—we used Vaseline or Kama Sutra oil, but I hadn't lubed him much—and his pubic hair became trapped in the mould. Jimi stayed in the mould for a long time, longer than we expected, but he was quite calm, cooperative, adaptive, and patient. "He was fucking the mold while waiting."

After the new deed, Hendrix and the band performed another gig before inviting the plaster trio to join them for a celebration. "It was not only significant because we were with them, but it was also the first time I had heard of an English band attending a party in Chicago." Graham Nash was there and I had no idea he was in town! It was really fantastic and unreal. My horoscope that day read, 'You rarely receive everything you desire in life, but today you will', and it came true."

In 1967, I performed in one of the first music videos, a short film promoting "Foxy Lady". When Mr. Hendrix revealed that he fancied teen-green me, I was too awestruck and virginal to yield to his palpable power. Cynthia had a similar reaction when the guitar god gave her the come-hither look. "Noel was more approachable and besides, he had that pixie/fairy look: hunched over and so pale with bad posture" . We both let out sighs, recalling the bright magnificence of hungry English musicians. "I had posters of him in my bedroom before they came to town, so I was prepared for him. He didn't come on strong—we arrived at the motel, and I ended up in his bed. He weighed significantly less than I did. I was double his weight. We had wonderful, simple sex. I was overjoyed that everything was going well with him. Cynthia and I agree that Noel was right at home under the sheets, teaching us both that sex could be a lot of fun and make us feel very good.

Cynthia was quite introverted, which most people find difficult to understand given the bold nature of her artwork. "Back then, I had a difficult time associating with the people I admired because I couldn't believe they'd want anything to do with me. I struggled with the big in-between: the capacity to relax and feel like I was on their level or that they were below mine—that took some time."

A few months later, the Experience reappeared, and Cynthia intended to cast Mitch but ended up in the sack beside him. "I slept with Mitch, and Noel was with somebody else" . Yes, there was a lot of sharing going on back then.

Eric Clapton was the impetus for a thundering, life-changing incident during another hopeful casting excursion. He recommended Cynthia perform as his band's opening act. "That was quite unbelievable! We discovered Cream's hotel and walked up to Eric Clapton's room. Dianne and I just chatted with him, and he was as polite as pie. We asked if he was interested in being cast, and he replied, "I might be, but I have a friend who may be even more interested—Frank Zappa." Deep down, I'm thinking, 'Ooh, isn't that guy a drug addict? But Eric took us to meet him, and he wasn't as intimidating and noisy as I expected. He was educated, respectful, and extremely curious, and he seemed intrigued in my notion of establishing a rock-and-roll museum."

When we realised we both had a drooling crush on Noel Redding, our high-pitched voices trilled and burbled over one other. Because of this and other thrilling discoveries, we knew we were rock sisters for life and couldn't wait to kiss and squeeze each other. I quickly made preparations to spend a wintry week with my newfound acquaintance in Chicago.

It was love at first glance. Cynthia was surprisingly modest and tender-hearted, and the pounds she'd gained on her small frame aggravated her already low self-esteem. I told her how stunning she was. We shared our deepest secrets, played a lot of records, and the days flew by, despite the fact that I was dressed completely inappropriately for the subzero, icy conditions. I recall my lips and toes being numb as I struggled through the slush in vintage chiffon and spike heels to watch Fleetwood Mac on New Year's Eve. We dribbled over Peter Green and laughed heartily at Mick Fleetwood's testicles, which appeared to be hanging out of his trousers as he bashed the drums. We later learned that he wore a pair of red wooden balls on his belt for good luck, but we didn't believe it for a moment. We sat about for hours, fawning about Noel Redding and other rail-thin rockers. Cynthia had hung a poster of the deadly new British quartet, Led Zeppelin, to the wall next to the canopy bed. "Just my type!" . I crooned, but Cynthia warned that they already had a very bad reputation. She should have heeded her own wise counsel, for shortly after I left, she met their scandalous road manager, Richard Cole, and had an encounter that left her sadly disoriented and confused. "I am keeping that big, juicy story for my own book. There was a routine that featured Robert Plant, John Bonham, and Richard Cole. Robert was the bait, while Bonham and Cole were the violent ones. Jimmy was always with a girl, which frightened John Paul." Let's just say Zeppelin lived up (or down) to their negative image.

"I felt like trash. It made me wary—it didn't make me want to stop being a groupie or Plaster Caster; it simply made me know that I couldn't enter any band's hotel room without first investigating them. To this day, I advise young girls to learn everything they can about a band before checking into their hotel room."

Cynthia was a fan of Eric Burdon and the Animals, but when it was time to go to work, she was confused by another massive crush. "I tried casting Eric, but the mould failed—and he wouldn't let me try again. John Weider, the guitarist, distracted me. He was helping me mix the mould, which caused me to mess it up. He turned me on, but I was too overweight.

Frank's sincere heart was in the right place, but when he brought her to town, Cynthia and La-La Land didn't exactly mix. "I loathed Los Angeles. The first week, I didn't like the folks I met; they didn't appear to like me. Put it this way: I hadn't laughed in ten days until I met Alice Cooper, who shared my Midwestern sense of humour.

Cynthia pursued playwright/actor/singer Anthony Newley and hired my friend Iva Turner as a player as a result of her teenage musical theatre addiction. "Cynthia was one of the few people I knew who loved Anthony Newley as much as I did", Iva explicates. "In fact, we agreed that I would be his plater if he ever wanted to be cast. So when she called and eagerly exclaimed, 'Guess who's coming over!' I guessed it on the first time and dashed to her flat. Mr. Newly arrived a few minutes later. He was adorable, sexy, and excited to be honoured into the Plaster Caster Hall of Fame. Following some introductory chit chat around the dining room table, Cynthia went into the kitchen and began scooping alginates, while I led our honoree into his bedroom. Cynthia counted down the seconds, 'Ten, nine, eight…', and when she got to one, the door seemed to blast open. Mr. Newley jumped to his feet, Ms. Plaster Caster held the container to his crotch, and they shoved his hard cock into the mixture. 'It's cold!' he announced. (Do not worry. I warmed him up later. Cynthia was a consummate professional. She gently removed his pubic hairs from the mould and commended him on a job well done. She knew right away that the cast was going to be good, and if you look at Mr. Newley's cast, you'll see that she was correct. It's a stunning display of her signature fusion of sex and art."

Her Hollywood apartment was robbed, and Frank's shyster manager, Herb Cohen, promised to store her valuable casts in his vault for "safekeeping". "I was passive and easily intimidated, I didn't want to argue: Frank trusted him and I trusted him, so I agreed" . As if being burglarized wasn't awful enough, she was hit by a car and severely injured while crossing the street on the Sunset Strip. At that point, even Mr. Zappa's passion was insufficient to keep her here. Cynthia wanted to go home. "Times were changing: for example, in Chicago, bands aspired to be cast, whereas in Los Angeles, they merely wanted to date attractive models. In 1971, the sexual revolution was shifting; people began to marry rather than sleep with strangers. I believe it was no longer trendy to be in my collection, so I didn't photograph folks like Jimi Hendrix. Everything went wrong at once; it was a truly bizarre time for me."

Cynthia returned to Chicago and went into a typical typesetting career, not producing any alginates for ten years. "I didn't like the '70s music. The rock was becoming too difficult for me, and I worked a regular job. Plaster casting is not conducive to the time I need to go to bed. Usually, the best time for a dick to go in my mould was 3:00 a.m., and I had to get up for work three hours later." Cynthia emerged from her semi-retirement in the early 1980s. "Punk rock started up and that's when the music got really exciting for me again" .

My debut book, I'm with the Band, was a success in 1986, and Cynthia and I were thrilled to be reunited for MTV's first sensational groupie exposé. "Even before I arrived in Los Angeles, the media jumped on the Plaster Casters, which surprised me. Slowly, more media gained fascination and began referring to me as an icon. I try not to think about it too much because it drives me crazy." Cynthia smiles. "However, it comes in useful when things are down. The fan letter keeps me going—it's quite helpful."

The Case of the Stolen Plaster Casts took five years to reach trial in a Los Angeles County courthouse, and Cynthia made the top page of the Los Angeles Times' Calendar section. "The casts were represented by exhibits A through Z. I know the paparazzi were there to photograph them. I had to testify about dicks on the stand for two days, and you, my doll, were my sole witness." Yes, I was a character witness for a genuine character, and even in the face of attempted character assassination, I was certain that the precious truth would triumph. A scrawny, fresh-faced bumpkin attorney displayed one of my previous "love letters" to Cynthia as proof that we had been lesbian lovers, saying that my testimony would thus be tainted. He mocked my flowery prose with C-minus drama.

"February 10, 1969: My true love, my dear piñata face, I love you and long to see you." Please come here to work. I adored your letter, my sweet. I'll need to write sooner rather than later because my heart is attached to the mailbox. If each lengthy mile between us was only a single kiss, I'd buy a distance ticket and wouldn't miss a single one. The judge was not going for it. Cynthia received her casts at the end of the four-day spectacle in which the bronzed penises in question stood gloriously in the sacred halls of American justice, and Herb had to pay $10,000 to return them to their proper owner.

Cynthia became an equal opportunity plaster caster a few years ago, when she began casting rocker girl's mammary glands. "I liked as many girl bands as boy bands, and girls were not only great singers, but also instrumentalists and songwriters, so it was long overdue." The first girl I cast was my friend Suzy Beal from L7, and it went perfectly. I've cast both sisters in the Demolition Doll Rods, the only band I have a full set of: Danny's dick, Christine and Margaret Doll Rod's tits. "I have Laetitia from Stereolab, Sally from the Mekons, and Karen from the Yeah Yeah Yeahs." Cynthia and I have discussed casting each other's titties in the future, which is an exciting prospect.

In 2003, the documentary DVD Plaster Caster: The Rock and Roll Adventures of Super-Groupie documented Cynthia's untamed life in art. Cynthia Plaster Caster was distributed by Fragment Films. I was interviewed, as was our long-time favourite, Noel Redding, who died shortly after the filming. "Before the shoot, he called me long-distance," she recounts, still struck by the distance between Cork County, Ireland, and Chicago, Illinois. "God, I'm proud and honoured and really sad, too, that his last appearance on film was in my cockumentary".

Cynthia established the Cynthia P. Caster Foundation in 2002, a legally sanctioned non-profit organisation whose aim is to provide financial aid to emerging musicians and artists. The foundation is funded through donations and the sale of Cynthia's amazing limited-edition art products, which include her art school sketches of the Beatles, the Byrds, Noel Redding, and Jeff Beck's crotch (you'll have to read her book for that story).

She has had art shows at upscale art galleries in New York and San Francisco, as well as funny spoken-word performances at progressive universities and rock clubs. We just had a rave-filled night together in L.A.'s Viper Room and thoroughly enjoyed ourselves.

Cynthia has now realised through pioneering artwork and burning soul-searching that she is not an extension of her mother, and for nearly forty years she has pulled the proverbial wool over her mother's cunning eyes. Amazingly, the ninety-year-old harridan is unaware that her infamous daughter is the notorious Cynthia Plaster Caster of Chicago.

Cynthia has been making ends meet for more than three years without having to work an insufferably restrictive nine-to-five. Cynthia Plaster Caster is her current sole source of income. "I feel more like myself. I feel more compact in my skin. I say whatever I want, and it encourages me to say more. "I have never felt more like myself than I do now."

Chapter 5: Love in Her Eyes and Flowers in Her Hair

I was dancing all over the dance floor at the Palomino club as the Flying Burrito Brothers performed their cosmic American music to a small group of loyal fans. Lost in the final notes of the strum and twang, a blonde sweet-teen noticed the glittery crucifix around my neck and kindly pulled me back to the smoke-filled honky-tonk. "I know you're wearing that cross because you love Jesus", her voice rasped. The chiffon-clad sylph quickly joined Miss Mercy and me on the floor, and as the evening went on, she and I fell in love in the way that only hippie-chick flower children could in the intoxicating spring of 1969.

I immediately wanted to touch her, and she reciprocated by stroking me with babysoft passion, her wide azure eyes beaming with happiness. After a few more songs, we dashed to the ladies room to learn more about each other, and it quickly became clear that she was there to see the Burritos' frontman, Gram Parsons. They had just returned from a romantic four-day trip to New York, and Michele was eager to see them again tonight. Unfortunately, it was not to be, as Gram had recently reconciled with his ladylove Nancy, but Michele put on a brave, lovely face and accepted it in stride. My beloved Chris Hillman wasn't giving me the time of night, either, so Michele and I kissed one other's rock and roll wounds and found bittersweet solace in our new friendship. The mischievous newbie from Manhattan and I immediately realised we were soul sisters, compatible spiritual seekers, and, eventually, roommates.

Before she danced with me at the Palomino, Michele had already dated Zeppelin's twenty-year-old singer during their first American tour. "When I first met Robert, he was staying at the Gorham, a second-tier hotel, and every groupie in New York was following him. "He was absolutely stunning."

On both coasts, word spread that the four guys in Led Zeppelin were far too risky. "I saw them at the Scene, and everyone said, 'This man Robert really likes you', but I was terrified by him because I knew every groupie, including the really hardcore ladies like Devon Wilson, was chasing him, and I didn't want to get involved. The night of their show, we were at Ratner's, a Jewish dairy restaurant next door, when Robert noticed me and approached me. 'Oh, here you are. Would you like to come see my etchings? He actually stated that to me. "He was just a boy, a man-boy, and I was slightly intrigued, but then they played, and afterwards..." Yes, indeed. When you saw Led Zeppelin play, everything was over except the orgasm.

Long before she met the Golden God, Michele had led an unconventional life, reared by her bohemian maverick mother in a modest Greenwich Village walk-up surrounded by hipness. "My mother, Gina, was clearly one of a kind, much ahead of her time, and faced a lot of criticism for her convictions. Being different back then required a great deal of courage. She was really stunning. I believe she was born strange. But, as nuts as she was, her children came first, so I always felt loved and cherished."

Michele and her older sister, Franny, never saw their missing father, and Gina prepared foods that Beaver Cleaver could not comprehend. "My mom was a spiritual seeker. She became interested in Zen Buddhism and was among the first New Yorkers to adopt a macrobiotic diet. When I was eleven, she became a vegetarian, and I grew up on brown rice.

Living with an unusual mother was not always easy for the girls. "When I was a youngster and my mother walked around barefoot, even in the Village, people made fun of her, which was embarrassing. But mom remained true to herself and raised us the best way she knew how."

At least Michele didn't have to sneak away to smoke her first joint. "It was kind of cool; I smoked pot with my mom once, and she said, 'You know, this is very nice, but I'm like this all the time.'" It was true.

Despite the fact that Michele was surrounded by music, I'm curious as to why she began to fall for artists. "My very first love, my first crush in kindergarten, was Elvis Presley" . I should have known, because I encountered Elvis at a very young, love me-tender age and never got over it. "I had thoughts of him coming to pick me up from class and wheeling me away on a cot. I even got as far as sleeping down on this temporary bed beside Elvis. "Pretty precocious, right?"

It only seemed logical that Michele's first love would be a musician. Ralph Scala was eighteen and Michele was fourteen when they started their love affair. "When you're first in love, the whole world revolves around this person —all your happiness hinges on them" . Ralph's band, the Blues McGoos, had a hit song called "Ain't Seen Nothing Yet," and he took Michele on tour with her mother's permission.

The band moved into the trendy residential Hotel Albert, which housed a slew of failing rockers, and Michele joined them. "I was literally fucked during lunch break and then trotted back to high school. And sexually, I had no idea how fortunate I was. I had no idea that not all men were as sensitive to their partners' sentiments. He was a great lover, and I still remember my first orgasm. I wasn't intending to have one, but all of a sudden, it felt like my insides were rushing out of my body, and I thought, 'So that's what everyone's talking about! I was 15 years old".

Steven's upbringing was similar to Michele's, and the two renegades quickly fell in love. "His father was a jazz musician, and his parents were frequently away, so Steven had the house just north of New York City, which became a popular hangout. We used a lot of drugs—nothing too severe; we took a lot of acid and smoked a lot of marijuana. The only time I used chloroform was with Steven. You apply it to a rag, inhale, and get extremely messed up."

Michele, 17, and Steven, 19, had a turbulent fling that lasted over a year. "Steven was a maniac; he was just nuts," she exclaims. "He had a lot of personality—one of those persons with no brakes, no filter, just complete id. He used to terrify me by squashing a banana with his teeth. He had a large mouth, and the goop would spray everywhere!"

I think Steven Tyler is one of the most attractive men ever, so I inquire about their romantic escapades. "He was the best lover." "He was the best," she assured me. "He lived in the attic on the top floor of the home. He had speakers on either side of his pillows, so when you lay down in bed, you were enveloped in a wall of sound. "He used to make this sexy blowing noise in my ear," she explains, making a delicate whooshing sound. "Yeah, I've got to give him full credit for being such a beautiful lover. He was incredibly liberated, both physically and sexually, and in tune with his body." Does she recall any of the music emanating from the pillow side speakers? "He used to play an album by the Hollies all the time, and now, whenever I hear that song 'Hey, Carrie Ann', I think of making love with Steven Tyler " .

The ribald ride became too much for Michele, and she spent less and less time romping in the gorgeous attic. "As much as I enjoyed being with Steven and was physically drawn to him—and the sex was amazing—I realised I wasn't in love with him. And the medications did not help either. In the end, it didn't fit with my romantic picture of how it should be. I wasn't even eighteen and far too young to be tied down."

Just a few weeks later, Michele dressed up in her suede Pocahontas mini to see the Flying Burrito Brothers at the Scene. "Oh my God, I adored their music." I played The Gilded Palace of Sin till my ears came off. The music was always what drew me in, and if the guy was as attractive as Gram, it didn't hurt! He had recently gone through a terrible breakup with his fiancée, and his heart was broken. He told me I helped him heal and was excellent for him. He was quite genuine. She exclaims, "Oh, he had this incredible skin, and those hands—oh my God, the most unbelievable hands I've ever seen."

When Zep returned to the United States for their second tour, a friend called to inform her she had run into "that guy Robert Plant" at The Scene. "He told her I was the only person in America he wanted to see. Of course, I felt flattered." Robert brought his wife to Los Angeles, but her visit was merely a momentary setback. "Sure enough, as soon as she left, I texted him, and he invited me to come over, and we began going out. Whenever he was in Los Angeles, he would phone me, and I was like his L.A. chick. The word spread quickly, and everyone knew about us. Sure, I knew he was married, but I was able to compartmentalise it. I didn't consider the repercussions and began to fall in love with him."

I had a similar experience while attempting to escape Jimmy Page's long-distance advances. And when he had his road manager, Richard

Cole, deliver me a note demanding my presence at the Hyatt House, I just tucked it away. But he got my phone number and gallantly invited me to their Long Beach gig, and my frail resolve crumbled.

"Remember when you bought this small gingerbread man dressed as an astronaut to give to Jimmy as a greeting gift? We hitchhiked down to Long Beach, and Richard Cole directed us to the side of the stage." We were the only girls onstage that night, and Michele and I vividly remember the incredible sense of being invited into that tempting inner sanctum. It was the headiest, swooniest rock and roll experience imaginable. Jimmy was about to delight the crowd, and when he noticed me, his angelic face brightened up. These were the heaviest heavenly moments in the globe. Michele agrees and laughs. "Yeah, and do you know what's funny now that we're discussing all of this? You're starting to look just as you did back then! It is true that your face has changed into that of an eager twenty-year-old."

She could never truly feel comfortable because the guy she adored was constantly at home with his wife and child, so Michele made sure Robert knew she had other partners. "I remember him ordering you to look after me and keep me away from the 'Flying Hot Dog Brothers' after I told him I was in love with Gram Parsons. "It was only half a lie, and Robert was married." Did she ever feel bad about the dishonest romance? "I was too young to properly comprehend the true impact. I was very naive. When he was with me, he was mine.

Robert wanted to meet Michele's mother, so when Zep played in New York, he called Gina and took her out to dinner with Jimmy. The two rockers and the madwoman from Greenwich Village got along well, talking about blues, jazz, and beat poetry. This interaction gave Michele hope that Robert was becoming more serious about her.

Waiting and yearning between tours didn't suit her, so Michele made the risky move across the pond. When Grandma arrived, I was already living in London with my trendy Granny Takes a Trip clothier boyfriend Marty. My adorable girl quickly discovered that her hero was already involved in yet another criminal affair. "The entire time I saw Robert, he was involved with his wife's sister. "How could he have been in love with both her and me?" I remind her that Robert was only a child back in those wonderful days.

"Yeah, a youngster at an ice cream shop," she says, "with all those flavours. "Why not have a double-chocolate dip with French vanilla?"

Some of Robert's beautiful songs were penned about his wife's younger sister. How did he juggle it all? When Michele had to leave for an appointment in London, Robert got romantic. "When I left, he told me, 'Little girl, I have a feeling you and I will be together for a long time. Don't you ever feel like that? I replied, 'No, because I don't want to be disappointed'. I'm not sure why I said that, but I remember it clearly. In retrospect, maybe I should have stayed instead of leaving for that dumb hair appointment. Who knows what could have happened?

When she complained about being a taboo subject, Robert bristled. "He said, 'That's not going to get you any closer to the altar,' and I was like, fuck you!" "How dare he be this cruel to me?" Michele is still bothered by her recollection. "I was completely devastated." Meanwhile, he was composing 'What Is and What Never Shall Be' for his wife's sister."

Michele saw her former rock prince only once more in London. "He took me to see some Moroccan jewellery sellers and said, 'I should get you something'. I realised that it was a goodbye gift. Then, when he drove me home in the cab, he murmured, "Hold me." I just want to remember what it was like. I remember seeing Michele, a wonderful, melancholy woman, standing at a bus stop on the King's Road in a dark grey rain, sobbing her heart out. "I was very, very heartbroken, as you know" . Yes, that was certainly a heartbreaker.

Michele finally travelled to Europe, where she spent a few years seeing the sights and driving men mad before returning to New York. Her amazing mother, Gina, who had become "Govinda" through a spiritual encounter with guru Meher Baba, died, and Michele was the one to discover her, slumped on the floor of her modest Greenwich Village walk-up. Michele sank deeper, and even her closest friends couldn't find her. But she never lost faith. Down deep, she remained the vivacious flower child I met at the Palomino. "I believe God—my higher power—was very helpful, as was deciding I didn't want to be a fucking casualty. I still respected myself and wanted to achieve something with my life, such as paint or write a book. I knew I didn't want to die without making a contribution to the world.

While a swarm of teenage dolls gave Michele the evil eye, she was dragged backstage like in the good old days. "Steven was overjoyed to see me and kept telling me how wonderful I looked. He grabbed my face and exclaimed, 'I can't get over you'. He looked so nice and sexy hugging me; his skin was like satan. We caught up on old times, and it was really great."

A few years back, Masters Page and Plant visited Portland, and Michele got up to some old-fashioned mischief. "I marched up to the call and announced that there were tickets waiting for me, since if Robert knew I was there, he would want to meet me. She took my name and returned five minutes later with two tickets and an all-access pass! The band played an excellent show, and Robert stated that "someone special was in the audience, bringing back incredible memories from long ago." Michele appears dreamy-eyed. "Being spoken about on stage after so many years was an incredible experience. I never expected to experience that kind of high again, yet it occurred."

Before Michele left that night, Robert made sure she remembered their time together. "He stated he couldn't understand why we hadn't seen each other, the squandered years, and the joy we could have had. It was incredible how he recalled everything—how we met, that my mother loved Meher Baba, and the Alice-in-Wonderland vest. He remembered the phrase he used to pick me up: 'Come up to view my etchings'."

As we get closer to Michele's house, I wonder how she came to be such a music fanatic and perpetual rock inspiration. "It couldn't have been a cultural influence or peer pressure since there wasn't any at the time; we were making it up as we went. We set the path for a lot of freedom that women take for granted and don't value. We were the first generation of women to freely show our love of music, and the music was obviously very sexual. But more than that, it was magical, and the magic was bigger than the bands that performed it."

I told her that some people perceived groupies as repressed and exploited. "But we were doing just what we wanted to do! We were in love with the music, and these men were the answer to our prayers. "They wanted us there and treated us like goddesses."

Chapter 6: The Virgin Groupie

I knew my buddy Cassandra Peterson for a decade before realising we had such similar rock and roll hearts. Few Elvira fans realise that the rib-tickling multimedia Mistress of the Dark was once an unapologetic groupie maiden.

Cassandra and I met at Ringo Starr's flamboyant 1980s event. The sumptuous grounds were frequented by manic-eyed Phil Spector, Roseanne Barr, my old label mate Alice Cooper, übergroupie Britt Ekland, and the pouty-lipped dead ringer for her father Lisa Marie Presley. I recall Cassandra being equally fascinated by the King's lovely kid, commenting on her facial expressions and familiar half-lidded stare as we ate skewers of big shrimp.

Pinning down the hardworking mistress has proven difficult because we are both such busy little beavers. She schedules our interview between a personal appearance at a comic book event and an Elvira calendar shoot. I've seen the vibrant redhead perform multiple times, wiggling around in her sensual Elvira disguise and enthralling audiences with her combination of caustic snarky and witty jokes. Above all, Cassandra is the archetypal comedian, and I'm excited about the prospect of capturing her witty, knowing nuances on paper. As we eat a meat-free, dairy-free lunch at the delectable new Real Food Daily on La Cienega, we reflect and wax nostalgic.

Like many of my committed groupie pals, Elvis was number one, but Cassandra's second boi-oi-oing moment came when she heard the Beatles. "My parents were big Elvis fans, so I grew up loving him. The first gift I remember receiving was '(You Ain't Nothin' but a) Hound Dog,' and at three years old, I choreographed the craziest dance you've ever seen. Then the Beatles appeared, and I became a Beatle geek. I saw them for the first time when I was eleven or twelve, and I forgot about them. I swapped all of my girlfriends at school since they didn't like the Beatles, and I celebrated Beatle birthdays with all of my new Beatle friends. I first liked Ringo, then George, and finally Paul. By the age of thirteen, I had fallen in love with John and remained with him. He was the only rock idol I had not met. And my favourite. I have met all of the other Beatles. "I suppose it wasn't meant to be," she sighed. "Besides, I am not Asian. And it is too late now.

The keyboardist for Mitch Ryder and the Detroit Wheels must have had the best gift of gab since he was the first rocker to entice Cassandra into his motel room. "I climbed into bed, stripped down to my bra and panties, and made out with him without allowing him to touch me. He contacted me for months, asking to marry me because I was the only groupie who refused to have sex with him. Being Italian, he believed that the only way to screw a nice Italian girl was to marry her, but I wasn't Italian!"

I understand the procedure of protecting the beautiful pussy since I've done it myself by perfecting the art of giving head. But Cassandra managed to keep her tongue virginal despite spending several hours in the sack with rock legends. "Yeah, but I'd put myself in situations. When I was sixteen, I had a horrific experience with Eric Burdon while he was on tour with War. I drove him back to the Holiday Inn, we were kissing, and he said, 'Come upstairs to my room'. So, like a doofus, I did. We joked around in bed, and as things become serious, I replied, 'No, I don't do that; I'm a virgin. Leave me alone. He said, 'You're kidding!' So he grabbed my car keys, slid them down his pants into his underwear, and said, 'OK, if you want your keys, come get 'em'. I chased him around the bed, but he refused to return them, so I rushed out the door, and he asked, 'Where are you going?' I said, 'I'm going to call the cops because you stole my car keys!' So he hurled them and hit me hard in the back with that sharp set of keys." Unfortunately, there's nothing like a rocker scorned.

This dangerous experience is memorable for another reason. "Jimmy's was the first penis I had ever seen. It was the longest, skinniest thing ever, resembling a snake or worm. But that night did not deter me. I kept getting myself into these situations."

Cassandra craved rock romance despite the fact that the Svengali guitarist had torn her aunt's mohair. I sobbed and pined. I was always in love with him, regardless of how he treated me. When Zeppelin came out, I was so smitten that I told everyone I had made out with Jimmy Page. I thought I was in love with everybody. I had a similar teasing relationship with Doug Ingle from Iron Butterfly. I also liked

Eric Brann, the guitarist with the small bowl hairstyle. I did this with band after band. I was madly in love after seeing them perform, so I had to go backstage and meet them. We'd make out, and I might let them feel me up. I had gigantic bazookas, which they adored. So I continued getting tossed out of hotel rooms, but I felt like I'd accomplished something fantastic.

For me, it was all about loving the music, and I know Cassandra feels the same way. "The music was so magical," she exclaims. "It wasn't really about screwing them. And it wasn't all about the celebrity. I had to like the music that they played. I met the Guess Who once and thought they sucked. I ate breakfast with them, but I didn't want to make out with any of them! The lead singer approached me, but he said something that made me stand up and leave the Holiday Inn coffee shop: 'We're going to be larger than the Beatles'. I was like, "Ha ha!" "Let's get out of here; these guys are too arrogant!"

While Cassandra was enjoying herself at the Denver Pop Festival, cops shot tear gas canisters into the crowd. Cassandra imitates everyone's voices throughout the story, including her own teen-queen falsetto. "One canister hit me in the head, causing a large lump and burning my flesh. The paramedics hurried me behind the stadium to rinse it off with boric acid. As I was leaving, a massive black bodyguard with a giant Afro said, 'Hey, you wanna meet Jimi Hendrix?' 'Yes, I do!' 'Come over here to his trailer'. So I go over, and there he is, dressed in his little costume. He asks, 'What happened to you?' And I said, 'The pigs were hurling tear gas, guy'. Jimi goes on a rage over America, saying he wants to leave and never return. "Fuck those bastards!" Are you okay? Let me see where they burned you. "He was really sweet." Jimi washed a cloth in cool water and carefully placed it on Cassandra's back, before asking if she wanted to share a joint. "So we start smoking weed and just keep talking. Then we kiss and make out, roll about, smoke, and have the best time. He never tried to be serious. They summon him to proceed, and he says, 'Here's my hotel phone number. Call me tonight so we can get together. I was concerned about what would happen if I went to the motel. Back to my seat, I told my girlfriend, 'Oh my God, Liz, you'll never believe…', but she snapped, 'Shut up!

Jimi Hendrix is about to perform!' I cried, "Listen!" "Here is his phone number!"

Cassandra absorbed more than a little bit of creative energy. When she was fourteen, she saw Elvis and Ann-Margret in Viva Las Vegas and knew she wanted to be a Vegas showgirl. "I thought about it constantly. People scoffed when I said, 'I'm going to be a showgirl in Las Vegas. I might as well have stated that I was going to be a Martian. Even my mother remarked, 'You can't be a showgirl; they have to be brilliant and beautiful'."

Cassandra had already moved out of the house, but when her parents planned a trip to Sin City, she begged to go. "We went to a big show at the Dunes, and because you had to be twenty-one to get in, I put on three hundred pairs of eyelashes and a million falls in my hair and tried to act sophisticated" . As they waited for the showgirls to appear on stage, the host approached the Petersons' table and asked Cassandra whether she was a showgirl. "I said, 'Uh... no'. My parents were letting me drink a glass of champagne, and I believed I was going to jail. He said, 'Stay right there' and proceeded to grab a woman named Fluff, who happened to be the dancing captain. She inquired, 'Are you in any shows here in Vegas?' When I declined, she asked, 'Would you like to be?'" Cassandra's family was moved to the nicest table in the house, and she was led backstage. Fluff had her do a few moves before telling her she'd be ideal for the forthcoming summer show, aptly named Viva Les Girls.

Cassandra's far-fetched desire was about to come true, but she was still under the age of eighteen, and her parents objected. "They yelled 'no way in hell' and hauled me out by my falls. I had only two or three months left in high school, and throughout the rest of my senior year, I vowed to run away and kill myself, until they said, 'OK, for God's sake, just get out of here!' The day I graduated, I packed my belongings into my Firebird and travelled to Las Vegas. I began rehearsals and became a showgirl.Elvis refused to accompany Cassandra to his kingly boudoir out of "respect" for her. "Elvis knew I was a virgin, and he was too damned respectful," Cassandra laments. "I could have kicked myself a hundred times for not..." Can you imagine? Unfortunately, I encountered Elvis before meeting the cad who devirginized me. "But we kissed a lot," she says, smiling. "I was so busy thinking 'Oh my God, I'm kissing Elvis, kissing Elvis...' that I don't even remember how good it was." We didn't stop talking from approximately two until eight a.m. the next day. He talked about spirituality, numerology, and religion, and I just listened. He had this odd hypothesis and wrote down a bunch of notes for me, which I still save. It was all about how numbers correspond to letters and how they spell various words like 'Christ' and 'Heaven'. And he offered me the most crucial advice of my life. After we sang together, he observed, "You have a good voice." Have you ever had singing lessons? I responded no, and he said, "You should get out of Vegas." If you stay here, you'll end up like one of these elderly showgirls. "You'll have nothing when you get older, and that'll be the end of you." Elvis advised Cassandra to take singing lessons immediately away and launch her own band. "If someone else had told me that, I would have thought they were full of garbage. But he was Elvis.

The very next day, she hired a vocal teacher, and a few weeks later, the showgirls in Viva Les Girls were called to audition for a number, and Cassandra was cast. "Not only did my earnings increase significantly, but I also became a featured player. From then, I travelled to Europe and became a singer in Italy. Elvis completely transformed my life. I thought I'd peaked, realised my dream, and achieved new heights. I truly thought I'd live in Vegas and be a showgirl for the rest of my life."

One scorching night, after Cassandra sang her new so-called lesbian song "A Good Man Is Hard to Find" with the rest of the sequined Les Girls, a renowned Vegas tycoon in tight glittering trousers came calling. "Our show was chosen the Best Show in Vegas. It was really stylish and hip at the time: a tits and feathers show. Tom Jones arrived and invited the showgirls to meet him and then party. I looked like a baby with my large round face, but he flirted with me and brought me beverages backstage. The other girls were in their forties, and one was forty, so I was new meat. Tom was gentlemanly and kind, so when he jumped on me a few hours later, I thought, 'Well, if I'm ever gonna do this, it might as well be with Tom Jones.'"I insist that you come clean. How was Mr.? "What's New Pussycat?" . Cassandra shakes her head and groans, "It wasn't a pleasant experience. It was terrible and horrifying. After that, I couldn't stop bleeding, and he replied, 'You'll be fine, don't worry. Here's some cash for a taxi. When I returned home and told my roommate, she said, 'You'd better go to the hospital'. I ended up in the emergency hospital and received a couple of stitches. Talk about having fun! I'm not sure if I was that small or he was that huge. Of course, I fell madly in love with him after that, and I assumed he felt the same way about me. I was sure we were going to run away together and marry! I went backstage to see him the next night, but he was with his two backup singers, the Blossoms, and was all over them. I was devastated. I recall sitting backstage in my dressing room for the next week playing that song of his, 'I who have nothing, I who have no one...'".

Cassandra continued to sing and fronted Mama's Boys, a band made up of seven gay men, as advised by the King. They were on the frantic disco circuit, performing in Provincetown, Massachusetts, when she received dreadful news. "I recall the exact moment I heard Elvis had died. It was quite heavy for me, just awful. Every night, I played a Joan Baez song, 'Never Dreamed You'd Leave in Summer,' dedicated to Elvis. I couldn't finish the song because I started sobbing. Of course, I wanted to see him again, but you could have probably contacted the Pope more easily than Elvis."

Cassandra, who has always loved music, quickly re-entered the rock scene after moving to Los Angeles. "Musicians are children in disguise—they just don't mature. Their lifestyles are so crazy; they're giant kids and so much more enjoyable to be around than regular guys with jobs." Cassandra rapidly secured her own position in the music industry as an A&R scout for Don Kirshner's Rock Concert television show. "I was a production assistant who checked out all of the new bands in town. It was the New Wave era, and for years I spent every night at the Roxy, Rainbow, or Whisky. I've seen every stinking band that exists."

During her time as an A&R girl, Cassandra continued to pursue a career in entertainment. "I segued from dancing to singing to acting and was doing stupid parts on Fantasy Island and Happy Days" . While on her honeymoon, she learned that a director was looking for someone to promote local TV horror movies. "He wanted someone witty and sensual, similar to the 1950s persona Vampira. When I returned, they still hadn't found someone, but becoming a late-night local horror movie host sounded odd to me. And it only paid about $300 per week, but I figured it would provide some income while I looked for more acting employment. I auditioned as myself, got the part, and had to create a look. My best friend from Mama's Boys created a picture of me with Ronettes' haircut, known as the 'knowledge bump'. He based my makeup on a Japanese Kabuki book and designed the black clothing to be as sensual and tight as possible. I pulled everything together and started doing the show."

Every October, it is impossible to contact Cassandra since she is so immersed in her saucy alter persona. The only way to see her is to go to one of her annual Halloween parties, and for several years I accompanied my son Nick to Knott's Berry Farm (Knott's Scary Farm in October). We were captivated by her high kicks and high jinks, which were interspersed with subtle double entendres and titillating music. Cassandra's career highlights would fill several pages; this doll is a self-taught genius. Along with her two hilarious films, Elvira: Mistress of the Dark and Elvira's Haunted Hills, she has made numerous television appearances and published a series of humour/mystery/horror novels. She introduced her own perfume, "Evil," as well as lines of greeting cards, confectionery, comic novels, bobble head dolls, action figures, and slot machines. Then there are the best-selling video and computer games, as well as Rhino Records' music collections. She has her own Elvira pinball game, a Revell ``Macabre Mobile" model car, and an unending supply of award-winning Halloween costumes and witchy accessories. She has been an active animal rights campaigner for many years, receiving PETA's Humanitarian Award in 1990. Cassandra makes numerous personal appearances each year, yet she still manages to fit rock & roll into her hectic schedule. "As Elvira, I opened for Mötley Crüe several times and cracked a few jokes, as well as Rob Zombie and Alice Cooper. I also presented U2 on their Zoo tour from Knott's Scary Farm." Was she ever tempted to return to her past wanton ways in the presence of so many rockers? "I was married for twenty-four years, but still flirts unmercifully with bands' ', she recounts. "It's sad because I had so many opportunities. I could have had flings like Elvira. I could have had anyone, but I was not on the playing field. "It's ironic," she laughs, "because I'm now too old."

Right. I'm sure the leather-clad fiend staring at her over his glass of squeezed greens would argue otherwise.

Cassandra may have romped with too many rockers, but she has no regrets. "Come on; it was fantastic. Sex is the best form of exercise, as it benefits both your brain and your blood! The strange thing about having many partners is that it's still OK for a person to boast he's had a million partners. But it's not acceptable for women. The birth control pill started to come out around the same time I did. Those small spherical dial packs changed everything. For most individuals my age, this fixed the entire problem. I didn't even consider sickness. I felt liberated; women were meant to have as much sex as men and enjoy it equally. But I would not recommend that lifestyle now."

It still irritates her that groupies were unfairly penalised for doing what everyone else was doing. "So we were wrong for screwing a group of guys in bands? My girlfriends were also screwing everyone, but the guys weren't renowned. It doesn't make things better, but it surely doesn't make them worse."

As we prepare to depart, "All You Need Is Love" plays over the speakers, igniting Cassandra's Beatlemania. "God, the Beatles were brilliant beyond magical," she murmurs. "They changed the whole world with their spiritualism, introducing the Eastern religion to the West" . When I tell her I finally saw my favourite Beatle, Paul McCartney, last year, she raves about his most recent live show in Los Angeles. Oh, Jesus. Unbelievable. The entire audience sang and swayed. It seemed like I was somewhere else instead of in the present. I had tears streaming down my cheeks. Seeing and hearing that level of greatness is similar to meditating. You're so concentrated on receiving energy from the music that there's no place for anything else to exist. It's similar to mountain climbing or other perilous activities. "You must be completely focused."

"There's a line by the poet Neruda," Cassandra says as we open the double glass doors into the West Hollywood heat. "'We only need to tell others who we are.'" That's what creativity is. These artists are telling us, "This is me, this is who I am; I am unique." And you can sympathise; you form a bond because you realise, 'Yeah, I'm like that too'."

Chapter 7: Absolute Beginners

By the time the brand-new cohort of young groupies came on the Hollywood scene, I had almost had enough of rock royalty. I was twenty-three years old, and while I still had my favourites, I'd discovered new fantasies to chase. Thanks to Keith Moon's generosity, I was able to join the Screen Actors Guild and star in two amazing B-movies: the innovative Massage Parlor and the timeless masterwork Carhops. I was sincerely studying acting and believed I was ready for my close-up. I will always admire the men who created rock and roll, but I badly wanted to tap into my own creative ability.

When I went to the Whisky, I avoided the slender prepubescents that littered the Sunset Strip in their mini shorts and towering platforms. I saw them more as an annoyance than a threat, even though one of them ventured to call me "an old bag" in front of Elton John one night. They teetered around in a pack, just like I had with the GTOs, but these brazen junior high teenagers were competitive and downright vicious, especially their acne-scarred platinum boss-baby Sable Starr. Queenie, Corel, Lynn, and Sable's closest confidant was a dark, gangly child with thick black locks who went by the name Lori Lightning.

I consider that night to be the low point of my career as a groupie. Jimmy's churlish actions marred an otherwise enjoyable seven-year rock frolic. I wanted to blame Lori, but she was only 13 years old. At her age, I hadn't even put away my Barbie dolls, and here she was, cavorting with a whip wielding heavy metal icon who was nearly thirty.

Lori is no more a lissome waif, but a bosomy, noisy force of nature. She exudes a genuine enthusiasm for life, and you always know when she's in the room. At Robert's aftershow party, I watch with amusement as she merrily whips her current lover while he clearly enjoys pandering to her every desire.

I've always been intrigued about the true tale behind her illicit connection with Mr. Page, and now that we're in the throes of Zeppelin nostalgia, it's the ideal time to revisit her promiscuous past. Lori, on a rare day off from her high-powered managerial position at the fashionable Theodore boutique, joins me for a few cups of English breakfast tea and empathy.

So how did such a baby girl end up half-naked in front of the Whisky a Go Go? "I got there by accident," Lori insisted. "Lynn and I went to school together, and she was friends with Sable." They were working at Star Magazine. That's how I got dragged in: Peterson Publishing noticed me. Lori was unaware of the dangerous allure of rock and roll when she became a pinup girl for lustful musicians. "I knew nothing. I was still a virgin and had no idea what was going on when they started putting makeup on me and dressed me up for magazine covers. The entire glitter rock era was decadent; that's when we really found our style and became bold. Platforms grew larger, skirts shrunk, and hair became wilder.

It was 1973, and many British bands had been on the road for years, so hotels and venues began to appear too similar. Despite having a woman (or three) in every location, rockers were becoming bored and appeared to seek ever-increasing and diverse stimulus. Keith Moon was driving town cars into swimming pools, while Mitch Mitchell spent the entire evening nailing his hotel room furnishings to the ceiling. Star magazine, which featured Lori and Sable, arrived just in time to help break up the monotony of touring. The underage glam-babies were a refreshing delight for jaded viewers.

How did Lori's mother handle her young daughter's rapid change? "It was especially challenging because she was a single mother. I had three sisters, and she was parenting us all alone. She was a waitress and worked every night, so we would sneak out and return before she arrived home. She didn't always know, but she eventually found out and went out to the Strip to ask Mario, the owner of the Whisky, 'Where's my daughter?' He soothed her, 'Val, don't worry; we'll look after her. "She's fine."

Back at the Hilton, the kids joined Stuie and David in their upscale neighbouring suites. "There was a large living room with fluffy white shag carpet, and Stuie rolled this enormous hash joint—one of those massive spliffs. I'd smoked weed before, but not like this. I got so screwed up. David entered the bedroom and announced, 'I'm going to take a bath. The door suddenly opens, and there stands Bowie, with his magnificent white complexion and carrot-red hair, no brows, and wearing a kimono. It was during his early Ziggy Stardust era that I realised, Oh, I want him. Sable threatened, 'I'll kill you if you go with him because I want him and you can't have him. He walked out and asked, 'Lori, could you come over here?' I replied, 'Alone?' I was stoned and paranoid, and he said, 'Yes, please, just you'. I walk in, he's ready to close the door, and I look at Sable, who is in tears. I was really nervous. I had boyfriends in junior high and did a lot of smooching, but I never had intercourse. So he leads me into the bathroom, removes his kimono, enters the bathtub, and sits there, staring at me with those different-coloured eyes. You must comprehend that he is stunning, with beautiful white skin. So he asks, 'Can you wash my back?' That was only the beginning. He knew it was my first time and was quite cautious with me. We began to fuck in every possible position. Then I told him how I felt about Sable, and he responded, 'Well, do you think we should go get her?' I nodded yes, and we moved into the living room, where she began fogging the windows and writing, 'I want to fuck David!' So he called her into the bedroom, where we all spent the night together. "David Bowie devirginized me."

Their passionate affair lasted more than two years. Except for the rare occasions when he was with Charlotte in London, Lori believed her knight in sparkling satin was loyal to her. "I was quite naive. I had no idea it could be any other way. I was a baby! He was a deity to me; it was like falling in love with Elvis Presley. I mean, when I went to the Forum, there were 30,000 people there for him, and he was with me. "He was twenty-nine when I was thirteen," Lori adds. "Do you know how old his wife is now?" Twenty-nine!".

How did it feel to get caught in that particular web? "It felt like being with the pope. You don't see performances like that anymore, enormous stadium concerts with a hundred thousand people. "And you don't see that kind of magic anymore, that great rock era—three nights at the Forum, thirty thousand people, with candles shining..."

To demonstrate that she was the one he loved, Jimmy asked Lori to listen in on phone calls he had with Charlotte. "He told me it was over with Charlotte and had been for many years. He'd call her and let me listen, so I wouldn't be concerned. He'd say, 'Charlotte, can you go fetch a number upstairs for me?' Instead of picking up the phone near the bed, she'd go all the way upstairs and take twenty-five minutes, then come all the way down and say, 'I can't find the number,' to which he'd scream, 'Why the fuck didn't you pick up the phone up there? "Are you stupid?"

Lori continued her successful teen modelling career in between Zeppelin trips. "I earned a few hundred dollars from a job, which I used to buy my small outfits—I needed money for platforms, after all! I had no idea what money was while I was dating Jimmy. He once sent me out to buy an outfit and paid me $300. I replied, 'I can't spend so much money!' I once coveted this stunning scarab necklace, and he purchased it for me. He liked me wearing long, flowy skirts. He wanted me to always seem like a gypsy—an innocent gypsy." What did they chat about throughout their extended time together? "Love," Lori exclaims. "I didn't know what else to talk about at that age! We fucked all the time, you know? I'm kidding, we talked about everything! He was so romantic and wonderful. I never thought of him as crazy since he was so possessive and protective of me. He wouldn't let me drink, and while I began smoking cigarettes, he went wild. He made me smoke an entire pack of Salems till I was gagging. I never smoked again. "He was like a father sometimes." For a few moments, we marvel at James Patrick Page's various sides. "And then, one day, I came across a photo of this transgender she-male, and I was like, 'What's this?' and he said, 'I wonder how it got there. "I'm not sure where that came from."

Lori had invited an attractive new acquaintance, model Bebe Buell, to join her and the band in New York. "She was my friend, so she brought her pet monkey and booked an adjoining suite with Jimmy and myself. "This is where everything goes wrong—Bebe was my guest." Oops. Lori returned to Los Angeles for a few days until the FBI cleaned out, then flew back to Pagey paradise. She had her own key to the suite, and as she walked in, expecting to fall into his slim, waiting arms, she was shocked to see Jimmy in bed with her friend Bebe. At least the monkey was nowhere to be found.

After experiencing grownup heartache at such a young age, she was resolved not to fall for another artist any time soon. "I suddenly realised I needed to grow up. I went from a radiant heart overflowing with love to a smashed bubble. "I shut down emotionally, physically, and everything."

Lori discovered that she still loved rock and roll as her heart mended, and she soon began cavorting freely with her favourite eager rockers. "Music was in my spirit. I was with David Bowie, Mick Jagger, Jeff Beck, Ronnie Wood, and Mickey Finn of T. Rex. I've seen Mickey on and off for years; he's another bad-boy freak. I went after terrible boys because Jimmy had been so nice and compassionate to me, and I needed to get him out of my system. I once did a three-way with Mickey Finn and Angela Bowie. I recall him hitting her ass hard before picking her up and throwing her into the air conditioner. I was hiding in the closet because I was terrified. I was wearing Angie's kimono and trying on her heels. They came in and grabbed me and shouted, 'Okay, get out now!' I was wearing her shoes with pom-poms, which she gave me. I had seen David Bowie on and off for years. I was in that entire circle, where you could either fuck a roadie or a rock star. I mean, sitting in a room with Ronnie Wood, why would you want to fuck the roadie? How do you turn that down? Ahh, Emerson, Lake, and Palmer. Obviously, I was with Keith Emerson. He was entertaining since he used to take me out on his motorcycle. Later on, I had a small thing with Carl Palmer as well! He was so attractive; he was a fucking god. I did have flings, but they were all fun; I didn't have another relationship for a long time because I couldn't get emotionally engaged."

One night, three Beatles, Stevie Wonder, and Mick Jagger all recorded there at the same time! Mick was having ego issues with John Lennon because they both wanted to sing and were Leos or whatever. I remind Lori that John Lennon was a Libra. "Well, Mick was having ego issues, so he was pouting in this back area with mattresses and shackles. I was there as well, escaping from the studio for a minute, when my friend remarked, 'There's someone you should meet'. She led me into the room where Mick was pouting." And how was her encounter with Mr. Jagger? "It was quite interesting. I assume he was high; he had some difficulty obtaining a hard-on and coming, but it was enjoyable. We rolled around, kissed and fondled one other, and had a great time. After that, I hadn't seen him in years until I travelled to New York to live with Freddie, the heroin dealer. Mick was there, so we had another brief fling. The third time I saw him was at Keith Moon's birthday celebration at the Beverly Wilshire. Mick entered the bedroom, and we had the wildest wild sex—he fucked me on the bathroom floor while Keith Moon and everyone else were in another room celebrating Keith's birthday! Bianca was downstairs while we were standing on the bathroom's marble floor. It was after she had surgery or something, and she was recovering at the Beverly Wilshire. People have always told me that I resemble her, which I find very nice. But I was never in love or serious until I met Jimmy Bain, who starred in Rainbow; he was probably the most serious lover I had after that horrible Jimmy Page nightmare."

The spangly, glam-slam glitter milieu was suddenly history, and Lori moved in with Mr. Bain and began working as an assistant to Deep Purple's Ritchie Blackmore. "The English Disco was what kept everyone together, and I believe it all broke apart when Rodney's closed—everyone went their separate ways. Times have changed; Star magazine has closed, Peterson Publishing has folded, and punk has emerged. That was when Sable relocated to New York with Johnny Thunders and the New York Dolls. I bailed because I preferred the rock scene. I was never into punk like Stiv Bators. I felt it was all nasty and ugly—I was never into heroin chic. It was also unfortunate for me because Jimmy became addicted to heroin during that time, which ultimately killed me."

Lori began working in the fashion world thanks to her modelling connections and gradually fell into an affluent Beverly Hills nightmare. "Everyone was trying disco drugs and getting high in the 1980s. I was heading to Daisy's, Pip's, and the Candy Store. Every night, O. J. Simpson would hang there; it was disco hell. After all, cocaine causes insane behaviour. Lori claims that in her early twenties, she became "responsible" after several acquaintances died. "I ran into John Bonham at the Rainbow one night, and it was the tipping moment for me. In his teddy-bear voice, he said, 'Lori, I've been coming here for fifteen years. I don't want to come back in fifteen years and see you still here. Something about Bonzo's comment struck a chord with me, and I looked around to see the same girls who had been on the Strip for years. I remember leaving that night and going out to find a job and get my life in order."

Lori has had numerous long-term partnerships, one of which resulted in her son Sean, who is now 19. "He's a terrific child. He surfs every day and aspires to be a professional surfer. I reared him, and he didn't need his father around. When I discovered I was pregnant, my AA sponsor told me, 'You have to leave your will and your life over to the care of God, and this is God's will for you. I had to eventually grow up, and that's when my life changed."

Fortunately, Lori has a wonderful relationship with her mother. "She knew I was meeting Jimmy since he asked my permission. I believe she thought my problem was little because she had three other daughters who were in problems. My sisters were dating low-riders and getting arrested for grand theft auto, but I was dating a rock star. "What could possibly be so bad?"

We've been talking for hours, and Lori needs to get to Pilates class. As she finishes her last cup of tea and gathers the gypsy skirts she still wears, I ask her how she thinks about the terribly tarnished G word. "I believe it has been degraded somewhere along the route, and it was never intended to be negative. Historically, groupies were band members' girlfriends. They were classy and sophisticated, but now the term "groupie" conjures up images of hookers and strippers. Pattie Harrison, Marianne Faithfull, Linda McCartney, and Anita Pallenberg were some of the groupies of the golden age of rock. They didn't provide blow jobs to go backstage—nor did we!"

Lori would not have missed a single minute of her passionate past, no matter how stormy. "I had such a monumental experience. I don't regret any of it. There was no AIDS back then, so you could explore freely. I constantly wondered, 'Why me? "Why did this incredible person choose me?" It was all very odd, and I felt quite fortunate to be there. I'm on stage, watching Led Zeppelin perform in front of 30,000 people—why me? Or I'm sitting in the studio with three Beatles, thinking, 'Wow, this is really incredible—why me?'"

Chapter 8: There's Only One Way to Rock

Fifteen years ago, while marketing my second book, Take Another Little Piece of My Heart, I faced the slings and arrows of Jenny Jones' jealous TV audience, expertly evading the venomous attacks. One furious middle-aged woman in Bermuda shorts refused to accept that her sockless hero, Don Johnson, had hung around with people like me. She argued that the images of us in my book were doctored, "touched up," she proudly declared.

I may not have had many fans in Jenny's peanut gallery, but I did have one on stage. That awful afternoon, I was joined by another rebellious groupie, the well-known Sweet, Sweet Connie from Little Rock, Arkansas. I was humiliated when she informed me on camera, in front of Technicolor America, that I was her hero and she had followed in my footsteps. After all, Connie Hamzy brazenly boasted to have sex with at least thirty music men in one wild night. What relevance does that act have to me? I was a one-time rock star seeking long-term love and romance.

After spending twenty-four hours with Sweet Connie, I'm embarrassed to admit that I was embarrassed that day. This straight-talking Southerner makes no apologies for her continued crazily wanton lifestyle, and I like her for that. Her lovely smile is genuine as she solemnly presents herself on a self-designed, sequin-splattered plate to musicians and their colleagues: roadies, soundmen, lighting guys, guitar technicians, managers, and promoters. Come on, everyone! These travelling men keep Connie's seemingly uncontrollable world revolving pleasantly on its phallic axis.

Back in swinging 1974, an intrepid writer from Cosmopolitan magazine ventured into a broken-down neighbourhood of Little Rock known as "Dogtown" to interview nineteen-year-old Connie at her parents' poor one-story home. As her tired mother, Joetta, hovered uncomfortably close, Connie gleefully boasted that she was already "taking care of two to three hundred people in the industry". This interview was conducted thirty-one years ago, and she has yet to appear on air. The writer recounts the shabbiness of Connie's teenage room, with the rag dolls on the bed and the hamster rattling around in its cage. Connie explained that it all began when she was fifteen and was invited backstage during a Steppenwolf show. She made eye contact with the band and paid close attention to the words of the song "Hey, Lawdy Mama," which was about "cock-teasing girls" who did not "put out."

"I kept thinking, wow, they're probably on a plane somewhere thinking, 'That Connie, she's just a C.T.'" And I resolved to reach out to the next group that arrived into town."

I couldn't fathom writing this book without including the most notorious groupie of them, Connie, and I've been looking forward to hanging out with her. But I've had to adjust my Little Rock travel itinerary a few times, which has made Connie concerned. By the time I book my flight and fly south, her unmistakable rasp has consumed a significant portion of my voice mail. Her abode is a shambles, she admits, warning me about her four nervous felines and subpar housekeeping abilities. She isn't persuaded I'm coming, saying, "I'll believe you when I see you, Paaamela". Up in the sky, I opened a recent Spin magazine and read an article titled "Oldest Living Confederate Groupie Tells All".

As I jump out of my rental car in Connie's driveway, the hot July air in Little Rock feels as sticky as cotton candy. She is nervously waiting for me on the tiny screened-in front porch, looking thin in skinny, tight shorts and a Van Halen T-shirt. "You did it! Come on in," she exclaims, before warning me about the state of her house, which I realise isn't too awful except for the pungent odour of kitty cat. Connie's cute little home is a little frayed and weird around the edges, but it's almost paid for, as she proudly boasts, presenting me her most recent mortgage bill as proof. She appears to be overjoyed that I've come to meet her, and I'm struck by the contrast of her world-weary guilelessness. The walls are covered in photos of Connie sitting on the laps of rock musicians, as well as autographed pictures, backstage passes, posters, laminates, and concert tickets. She grabs the remote, wanting to surprise me with a video of our old MTV groupie interviews, but when I decline, she is unhappy. "I'd rather go to your local haunts," I tell her, and after worrying that she might miss an important call from "Edward Van Halen," we head to Bennigan's, which is not far from her home on Green Meadow Drive.

We step onto the barstools, and boiling over, she takes my first book from her bag, introducing me to the owner, the bartender, and a handful of other patrons as a "famous writer" who has come to town expressly to interview her. Connie's excitement is contagious. Even when people stare at her dismissively, she enjoys the attention and laughs, "We were on Jenny Jones together!" She orders her first white wine of the day and doesn't stop drinking until well after midnight.

I ask her, while she sips her chardonnay, how she became so interested in music. "I was an only child, and I believe that's why I became a groupie. I'd always wanted an older brother, and now that I'm a groupie, I have many! Even before puberty, in the fifth and sixth grades, I went to watch the Dick Clark Caravan of Stars. Sam the Sham and the Pharaohs, Paul Revere and the Raiders, and the Yardbirds performed. I often saw these attractive women backstage and thought, 'I don't want to be out here with all these people. "When I get older, I'm going to do that, and I'll be back there." In ninth school, Connie was brought backstage at the fatal Steppenwolf concert, where her controversial future was sealed. Her companion joined up with singer John Kay, while Connie ended up with drummer Jerry Edmonton. "I was a virgin at the time, but he did convince me to take off my shirt. I said, "I'm on my period, and I can't do anything because I'm a virgin," to which he replied, "Have you ever heard of oral sex?" I asked, "What does that mean?" "Talking about it?" She eventually discovered that her rock conquest did not relate to public speaking, so she swiftly began studying the delicate skill of giving head.

Following Steppenwolf's anti-cockteasing lyrics to the letter, Connie was determined to "put out" for the next band to visit town. The drummer for Detroit's Frijid Pink gladly removed Connie's virginity barrier and was the fortunate recipient of her newly acquired oral knowledge. The soon-to-be Sweet Connie went on her way.

After finishing her glass of wine, Connie wants to take me to her favourite hangout, the Canyon Grill. The bartender serves wine for Connie, who introduces herself and flirts with two young cops. Then we continue where we left off. "After Three Dog Night, word spread because I had to blow and screw promoters to get to roadies and past the building's security. I started at the first floor and worked my way up."

Seeing backstage stickers on guitar and amp cases gave her a fantastic idea. "I went to a printer in Little Rock and had five hundred paper stickers produced that read 'Connie in Little Rock — 501.753.1005', and you know what happened? The first set was taken off, and some jerk plastered them all over town, and people phoned my parents to inquire, 'What's this?'" How did her family deal with her growing popularity? "They did not have a clue for a long time — until the song came out, and then they began to get wind of it". What did they believe all the men were talking about? "Selling cookies for the Girl Scouts, I guess —and I sold candy for the Future Teachers of America".

Her parents couldn't keep her at home, so conquests came quickly and furiously. She had a great time with Grand Funk Railroad, and she "got it on" with all of the Chicago members while everyone watched. The same thing happened with the Allman Brothers. Connie's trip out of town with her mother backfired when she found they were staying at the same hotel. "The Allmans stayed there for a few days. I completed the roadies. I did everything. They were all amused to learn that my mother was only upstairs. When we returned to Little Rock, she informed my father that it had been a real picnic. 'You mean all she did when you got there was chase the bands? I sent you all over there to take her away from them! I can't do anything with her! We might as well throw her in a juvenile facility or send her to the nuthouse! They threatened that repeatedly."

Concert organisers took advantage of Connie's oral generosity and began inviting her to perform in adjacent cities. "They flew me to Oklahoma City to see KISS, then to St. Louis to see the Who, where I met Keith Moon for the first time. I was flown to Shreveport to watch Alice Cooper. I began fucking him really early in the game because I would go to Memphis to meet him."

Gene Simmons, the monster bassist for KISS, is a long-time friend of mine, and I'm intrigued about his bedside manner. "He was quite good. He is well-endowed, but you know what? I had severe anorexia at the time I met him, and he spent a lot of time chastising me for my weight. I was never with Ace Frehley. He got intoxicated and flung a room full of stuff out of the hotel room next to mine. I fucked Peter Criss, Paul, and he was fantastic! He told me I had a clit like a small dick. But after I hooked up with Peter, it was always Peter from then on."

Connie and I had more in common than we expected, including Waylon Jennings, Jimmy Page, and Keith Moon. She met the bright, crazy drummer for the Who when a promoter invited her backstage in St. Louis. "I was in the dressing room after the show—security wasn't what it is today—and Keith and Roger weren't getting along. Roger decided to upend an entire table full of food, and then he began crying. Keith and I began fooling around, and before I knew it, he had taken my jeans off and was fucking me with a banana to lighten the situation and relieve the tension. Keith was the type of guy. After seeing someone get raped with a piece of fruit, you forget what happened five minutes ago! Then he said, 'Come back with me to the hotel', and I spent the night with him in the Chase Park Plaza. The entire time I was with Keith, I thought, 'This is the guy I used to see on Where the Action Is! He had the most stunning facial characteristics as he was playing the drums. When we weren't making love, he had a small 45-rpm record player and played a stack of records while singing along to them. He'd go down to the bar for drinks and bring them back up to the suite, where we'd sit and drink, sing, and fuck. We sang 'This Diamond Ring' and 'Love Potion Number Nine' at the top of our voices. He urged me to accompany him to Detroit, but I answered, 'I can't. "I live with my parents and don't have any clothes."

Connie and I have my early mentor, Frank Zappa, in common, but in a very different way. He was always drawn to unusual people, so their encounter is not surprising. "Gosh, I only saw Frank once, but he was such a nice guy—and he was so sorry. When I first saw him during the sound check, I was joking around with the crew because they had looked after me all day and given me a break. I was heading with his roadie into a small tuning room when Frank took the microphone and said, 'Okay, Connie, I guess that makes number 10'. He turned out to be an excellent lover, and one night in his hotel room, he remarked, "I want to apologise to you for saying that."

When Connie was almost nineteen, two things happened that forced her to leave her childhood home. "Not much had happened with Grand Funk other than me blowing Don Brewer and Mel Schacher up, and if I recall correctly, I took care of the piano player once or twice. In June 1973, I was sitting on a towel at the beach, listening to my transistor radio. Most of my girlfriends were out on rafts in the lake when the disc jockey remarked, "Ladies and gentlemen, we just got the new song by Grand Funk Railroad, and you all are not going to believe this—you know that dark-haired girl you always see backstage at concerts?" "When I heard the first few lyrics of this song, I started jumping up and down, screaming for my friends to come listen."

On our journey back to Green Meadow Drive, Connie shocks me by suggesting we visit the Little Rock Zoo. She appears to be responsible for maintaining a tiny vegetable garden on zoo grounds. "I was a wonderful teacher," she adds as we look into the cages at the small animal refuge. "They prevented me from doing it because of who I am, and I have the press to show it. The students loved me, but they didn't want me to teach at school since I'm so controversial. "I am who I am, and that isn't going away." She tells me about her part-time work, which surprises me even more. "Well, Pamela, I rent wagons and baby strollers here" . In truth, her small vegetable garden is hidden under rows of shiny rental buggies. She walks over to a leafy plant and, beaming, unveils a large, red tomato.

Back home, Connie shows me her favourite picture of bright-eyed elementary school students and tells me how "precious" they were to her. "But I have dedicated my life to being a groupie!" she exclaims, as wine gurgles from the faucet attached to a Gallo box in the fridge. "Thank you! You started me. "It is your fault!" I told her that she was trailing Dick Clark's fresh-faced caravan before I ever penned a line of I'm with the Band. "I know one damned thing: that's when I realised that the broads backstage looked a lot more comfortable than I did out there in a pile of people" .

"That was the first time I had caviar—with Led Zeppelin when I was nineteen. I'll never forget the large tuna-salad fish mould topped with black caviar. And I don't even like caviar! Sex with Bonham was fantastic, and he kept insisting, 'I'm not leaving Dallas until I get that

'Vette. I'm going to have them place it on the back of a truck. I'm going to take it to California and drive around. And he got what he desired. Did she ever see Bonham again? "No, I didn't, but I did see Keith Moon after that and told him I'd been with Bonham and he said, 'We're gonna do something together eventually'" . Unfortunately, the confluence of outstanding minds never occurred.

She's been talking to me all day about Doe's, a laid-back neighbourhood hot spot and popular Clinton hangout where the owner is taking us to dinner. "Who knows?" she sneers. "Clinton's in town; he might even be there" . Connie promises to reveal the specifics of her encounter with our former charismatic President of the United States over a massive plate of garlicky shrimp.

After looking at the photos of the attractive president with local celebrities on the restaurant walls, I toast Connie with a glass of wine, and soon we're chatting with a table full of travelling sales people sitting next to us. She, of course, tells them all about why I came to town, and it turns out that one of them had read my works. We both sign autographs and pose for photos, feeling like divas in the diner. Crustaceans are delivered, and as we dig in, Connie launches into an anti-Clinton tirade. I quickly realise that she does not share my admiration for William Jefferson Clinton.

"I occasionally went to the bar at the Riverfront Hilton for happy hour, and the manager said, 'If you're a regular here, you're more than welcome to use the pool!'" Rush had stayed there a few days before, and we all partied around the pool. Anyway, I was the only one out there that day. There were no bands, and everyone was gone. I was in my bathing suit, writing in my diary, when two males approached me. One of them used to live near me, and he asked, "Connie?" I assumed it was you. It's Mike Gaines. I used to be your neighbor. I'm currently working for the governor's office. Then he said, "The governor wants to say hello to you." I responded, "Well, Mike, I met him before, at an Olivia Newton-John concert." He said, 'He wants to say hi to you again', and I said, 'I don't have any clothes on. He answered, "That is exactly why he wants to talk to you." Connie tossed a towel over her shoulders and followed Mike inside. "Clinton is standing there, saying, 'I just want you to know you made my day by laying out there in that tiny purple bikini. Do you have a room here? I replied, 'No, Governor, I don't. He asked, "Are you sure you don't have a room?" I said, "No, Governor, I just snuck in to use the pool, sorry." He said, "Well, where can we go?" He unlocked another door and said, 'We can't go in there.' Then he opened the doors to the laundry room, and we went in and began groping and fondling. I caressed his cock—he's extremely endowed—and just as we were ready to get to it, he moaned and someone stuck her head out from behind the washing machine. He said, 'I guess we'd better get out of here'. We moved back into the hall, and he asked, 'You going be here later?' I replied, 'I'm gonna be here all afternoon, Governor. He said, 'I'll call or come back. I have to be up in the Capitol to direct the legislators. I swear to God, I never addressed that cocksucker as anything other than 'Governor'. Later, I go into the pub and tell the manager about it, and he responds, "Yeah, I know, the governor is a whore dog."

I'm curious as to why Connie is so vehement about the Clinton controversy. Apparently, Big Bill later denied that it had happened, and Connie values honesty. Her mother advised her to keep quiet, but the story about the groupie and the governor quickly spread, and the Arkansas Democrat-Gazette published it on the first page. The right-wing American Spectator requested Connie to take a lie detector test after the governor's staff denied the allegations. "They were so eager to get his sorry fucking ass that they said, 'We'll pay if you do it,' and I said, 'Hey, I've got the balls to take it.'" They stated there was a 50/50 possibility I wouldn't pass, and I had to deal with that. I smoked marijuana, drank wine the night before, and told the polygrapher exactly how much I drank and how much I smoked. I said, 'Look, I was nervous, but I guarantee you, I'm telling you the truth. They gave me the test three times, and I passed each time."

Fortunately, Connie had always been listed in the phone book, and shortly after her engagement ended, she received an unexpected call from a certain raconteur. "He said, 'Connie, this is Jimmy Page', and I said, 'I don't believe you'" . Jimmy called Phil Carlo, a record executive she knew from working with John Bonham. "He said, 'Connie, it's Phil—that was Jimmy. We want you to come to Dallas. He's on the ARMS tour, and we'll prepay your ticket. "I was substituting that day and left for the airport when school let out." Connie spent the following three days swapping rooms with Jimmy and Phil. "I did irritate Jimmy since it was during my anorexia stage, and Phil called me aside and said, 'Jimmy does not want you throwing up in his suite anymore'. When I got engaged, my anorexia became more apparent. I was divided between what was right and 'I wanna keep doing what I wanna do!' I figured, 'I'll just kill myself'. It didn't work, but it got people's attention." Did she continue to have ribald interactions with Jimmy, even if he didn't want her hurling in his suite? "Yeah, as much as I could, but I mostly gave him the head. "He was doing a lot of nose candy." Connie pauses to light a bowl. She gives me a hit of pot, but I have to decline because I'm at work. "Most of the time I was with Jimmy, he was complaining about Robert. And I know what they were arguing about: blaming each other for Bonham's death. But Phil was fantastic".

When her father died in October 1984, with bad blood still brewing, Connie drowned her sorrows with another pop singer. "Rick Springfield came to town, so I guess I needed to let my hair down. It was my first gig since my father's death, and Rick and his team treated me well, giving me passes and allowing me to stay out in the dressing room. I hit it up with his massage therapist, and they prepared a movie to watch on the plane. He was Dr. Noah Drake on General Hospital. It was just something to take my mind off the fact that we had buried my father, and two days later, my mother stopped speaking to me."

Connie Hamzy may have reached the ripe middle age of fifty, but she has no plans to behave like an adult anytime soon. "As long as I can, I'll do it, but hell! Now I need to pace myself a little differently. But I plan to make up for missed time this weekend. Okay, so I know where Dylan and Willie are coming from—they're playing Memphis the night before they play Little Rock, and they'll be leaving Memphis and arriving at three a.m. Tommy, the guitar tech, said he wants to come over here because he doesn't have to start working on both guitars until about two p.m., and I live near to where the gig will be. When his bus arrives, I'm going to jump up and race over there to get him, then bring him over here. On Friday, I'll go to the zoo, collect my check, water the garden a little, then go to the bank, cash my check, come home, and sleep as long as possible till Tommy calls and says, 'The buses are here, come get me!' "After we fuck around, I'll take him back to the gig and spend the rest of the day and evening with him. I'd really like to go with him on the road because on the Fourth of July, Willie Nelson has his picnic in Fort Worth..."

Sweet Connie is naturally excited to get back on the road.

Chapter 9: Crazy, Crazy Nights

It's a damp, grey afternoon in Seattle, and I'm sitting in one of the city's countless rustic coffee shops, waiting for a captivating woman I met on the Internet to arrive and tell her wanton stories. Gayle O'Connor appears to be a seasoned, unrepentant, music-crazed motorcycle lady based on her email correspondence, and I can't wait to revisit her 1970s groupie days. I had just ordered my second chai tea when I heard the unmistakable booming vroom vroom of a huge motorcycle. I look out the window to see Gayle jump out of the fancy Harley-Davidson, remove her helmet to reveal short, spiky golden hair, and stroll purposefully inside the coffee shop. I'd informed her about my ridiculously red hair, and she recognizes me as soon as I arrive at the bottom of the stairs to greet her. Gayle is dressed completely in black leather. Her eyes shine and crinkle at the corners, and her teeth are astonishingly white. She extends a hearty, solid handshake, and her grin draws me in.

She gets a large black coffee, and we take our drinks to a quiet table upstairs. Gayle speaks in short, clipped phrases and laughs loudly and freely. She takes off running after my first query.

"My first rock-and-roll memory? I was nine years old, sitting in my sister's bedroom, listening to early Rolling Stones songs like 'Paint It Black'. In 1968 and 1969, we lived in Laos. My father served in the Vietnam War. He was with the CIA and Air America, going into the bush to teach the men. He was a wild alcoholic, and there was a lot of drinking abroad. In Laos, there was only one radio station, which broadcasted for an hour every Sunday. The bathroom was the only place we could get reception, so we'd sit there and listen to American music. The soundtrack to Easy Rider was my first must-have album. And the Beatles' White Album had just been released. My first concert was the Monkees. Peter Tork was my first rock-and-roll crush. Micky Dolenz came to my high school's homecoming game years later, although it was no big deal at the time. I was probably smoking cannabis.

"I was the rebel in my family, although my mother thought I was really good. I am in the middle. My two sisters and brother were constantly together, while I was well over on the other side. They'd always tell my mother, "Gayle is the worst." You're not sure what she's up to. They began to distance themselves from me while I was in my adolescent years. My little sister thought my elder sister could walk on water. My brother was full of teen angst because my parents had split up. My father disappeared and did not contact us; no Christmas cards, no presents, nothing. Following that, we were primarily raised by two women, with no male presence. Alice Cooper said, "My first concert was here in Seattle." It was 1973 and I was a junior in high school. I went with my buddy Michelle, and I had a blue halter dress that my mother wouldn't let me wear, so I changed on the way. I had a large star painted over one of my eyes with glitter. Somebody from Alice's entourage got us passes, and we ended up backstage. They were on their way to Vancouver and remarked, 'You girls should come to Canada'. So Michelle and I packed our bags and caught a ride to the border. However, we were not permitted to cross because we did not have concert tickets. We replied, "Oh, no, no." We're with the band. But the border patrol answered, 'Sure, right' and sent us out. So we walked into the woods in our giant wedgie platform shoes—mine were green snakeskin—and kept going north, north. We hid whenever a car passed by and remained in the woods. Swear to God! And I was just seventeen. We eventually hitchhiked and found a ride to the Bay Shore Inn, where the band was staying. It was the middle of the night, and we came across a couple of roadies in the foyer. Bottom line: my companion ended up in one bed, while I ended up in another. I wasn't a virgin, but I'd only slept with about two males. I guess I was prepared to accept the rock and roll experience because I didn't say no. We acquired Alice Cooper tickets, partied hard, and returned home.

"That was the beginning, and once I got started, it was game on. I needed to do it more because it made me feel important. It was incredibly intoxicating. The guys were famous, and I was with them as we entered and exited limos. I guess they were only flings, but I wanted more. I wanted to be their girlfriend, but I didn't approach it correctly. My second major groupie experience was with Bad Company. I was with Phil Carlo of Atlantic. He was a gorgeous dude. I joined them in San Francisco and then travelled to Arizona with Phil for a few weeks. He was on a sabbatical and called to say, 'Do you wanna join me?' We rode horses and stayed at the

Camelback Inn, where we sat in the pool and drank. What a life. Oh, and Mick Fleetwood was one of my first big names. I am ashamed when I look at images of him now. He was one among my first large ones. He was at least 20 years older than me. "That was before I became picky, but he was very nice, so I don't want to say anything rude." My first job after high school was selling clothes at JeansWest, a fashionable apparel boutique. I robbed them blindly. When I was nineteen, I quit my job and began topless dancing. I was making a lot of money stripping, enough to sustain myself on drugs and alcohol. During that time, Kansas came to town, and I met with their manager, Jeff Glixman. He was stunning, with a large nose and long, wavy hair. It was the first time I tried MDA, the modern kind of ecstasy. It didn't matter whether I was with a roadie or a manager; all I wanted was to be a part of that scene and stand out from the crowd. I wanted to be special, and I was. It was such a fantastic existence. I would be very heartbroken when they went and vowed to call. They would occasionally do so, but not always. But sometimes I received exactly what I wanted, and then I moved on. "It was power." I had a wild night with Stephen Stills in Los Angeles. He was unpleasant, and we had a bad time. He was fairly raw. But he was also really disrespectful afterwards. He was excellent when it benefited him, but later he turned hurtful. He was one among them. I stayed the night, but the next day, he was finished. I had a crazy night with Davy Johnstone of Elton John's band. He apparently dated Kiki Dee for a spell. I recall being in bed with him and sitting on top of him while he was on the phone with Miss Dee. I remember thinking, 'I am so it right now!' I felt comfortable about a lot of the guys. I spent one night partying with Peter Frampton's group. There was Barry Brandt from Angel and David Flett, the guitarist from Manfred Mann, who I had a terrific time with. But before they got to town, I knew I had to get Roger Earl, Foghat's drummer. I answered, "That will be mine somehow." I'm not sure how, but that will be mine. There was something about him. "I learned to go to the local radio station for band interviews." I went backstage to meet Chicago. Walter Parazaider, one of Chicago's sax players, was a big influence on me. I have images of him in boxers with a small plush Pooh bear. He was quite married. Many of them were quite wedded. Ringo Starr attended a celebration for Chicago. And, for me, the Beatles exist in another world. I dated George Harrison's road manager or public relations representative, I can't remember which. I was in the car with him when he stated, 'I need to stop at George's house. It was up in the hills. He told me the story about the stolen street signs on Blue Jay Way. When we came in, I found myself standing at George Harrison's house—in front of one of the Beatles! He was very pleasant and polite. I wasn't sure if I could say 'Oh my God!' I didn't because I was acting cool. Oh, and Alto Reed was among the best. He was a member of the J. Geils Band as well as the Silver Bullet Band, which featured Bob Seger. He was wonderful. He was quite real. No male had ever told me my bodily parts were attractive. I'll never forget this. I have felt ashamed since I was so young. He sat down between my knees, touched me, looked at me, and then looked into my eyes, saying, "Just look at it." It's beautiful. He taught me how to be vocal and communicate during sex. I just got goosebumps thinking about that. In 1976, KISS arrived in town. I first slept with Paul Stanley, then with Gene Simmons. Gene was great! He is very intelligent and nice. He's just real. We had a wonderful experience. I hung out with him at the Sunset Marquis, and they left three weeks later. I lived with Debbie. The telephone rang, and it was Gene. I asked, 'Hey, what's up?' I was nodding to Debbie and said, "Oh my God, it's Gene!" He replied, 'We're taking a vacation before we finish the next album; would you like to come to New York for a couple of weeks?'

Did I take him up on it? Yes, of course. Did he pick me up from the airport? No, absolutely not. He was staying at Riverside Drive. I arrived there, and I was dying! We went shopping, visited restaurants, and did regular things. It was during KISS's makeup era, so we could simply walk down the street. Now, he was wearing six-inch platforms and skull rings on all of his fingers. He had skintight jeans and was really tall. Nobody knew him, yet he still appeared abnormal. The night I recall most vividly took place at a well-known restaurant. We went to the door and discovered a private party for Hall & Oates. So the doorman said, 'I'm sorry, but there's a private party'. And Gene very eloquently replied, 'Oh, well, thank you anyhow'. We began to walk away when the doorman asked, 'Hey, wait a minute, aren't you Gene Simmons? Oh, you can come in! I was twenty years old, and this room had Rod Stewart, the Rolling Stones, Hall & Oates, and Bad Company. I was standing next to a cigarette machine, my heart beating, thinking, 'I can't believe I'm here! And I was with Gene, so it was a big night.

"Gene knew I'd already been with Paul Stanley, but he didn't mind. And did Paul care that I ended up with Gene? No, he did not. These were the days. Gene took me to the studio one afternoon, and it was my first time hanging out with Peter Criss, and we instantly clicked. Gene was quite square. When I had a glass of wine at dinner, he would ask, 'Are you okay to talk? To walk? You've had some wine. So, after the seminar that night, Peter and his wife, Lydia, joined us for supper. Well, the chemistry between Peter and I was simply raw. We returned to Gene's place after dinner. When I went to get a drink, Peter followed me into the kitchen, and it simply happened. We were all over each other like flies on garbage. With Gene and Lydia upstairs! I was about to leave in three days and wondered, "What am I doing?" I'm in New York with Gene, and I'm making out with Peter. Oh my God, what will we do? So we go back upstairs, and I attempt to remain cool. I was in bed with Gene at 5 a.m. when the phone rang. He answered the phone and handed it to me, saying, 'It's for you'. It was Peter asking, "Can you get away?" I will meet you downstairs. Gene turned over and fell back asleep, so I got out of bed, went downstairs, jumped into Peter's sports car, and we drove away. We stayed at his manager's residence for three days. It was an extremely white New York apartment. We fucked our brains out, ordered in, and did a lot of blow. Oh, Peter got off the hook. And hung like a horse. Peter was enormous! Oh, it was on! I called Gene, and he said, 'I believe it's about time you came to retrieve your stuff, huh? He was cool. I went and grabbed my stuff, and Gene is still really cool to me today.

"Typically, I partied with roadies and managers, simply having a wonderful time. My pals would ask, "Why are you hanging out with him?" He's only a roadie. I wasn't starstruck enough to sleep with someone I thought was a jerk. If David Lee Roth had been nicer, I would have slept with him in a heartbeat! But he was an asshole. I was a dancer at the time and had attended a Who party. Another woman there was also a stripper. Roger Daltrey went to her and said, 'Why don't you fucking dance for us?' I looked at him and replied, 'Why don't you fucking sing? She isn't working right now! He was cocky and confrontational, just like David Lee Roth. They believed they were God's gift. Roger Daltrey? An asshole and short! But that night, we were all out partying, which was quite crazy. Keith Moon sat next to me on the bed, locked my eyes, and proceeded to act out the Randy Newman song '(Beware of the) Naked Man'—'Old lady standing on the corner/middle of the freezing, cold night.' He was so insane. He placed his room key in my hand, curled his fingers around it, and said, 'Be there in an hour'. I replied, 'I don't think so,' and handed it back to him. I started talking to Pete Townshend, and I could tell he was interested in me. That night, I chose Pete, and he was absolutely insane. I was wearing red cowboy boots that I bought at Nordstrom. He scooped me up and took me into the shower. He turned on the water, and we stood against the shower wall. I had my fucking red boots on and they got torn, which I'll never forget since Nordstrom took them back! Yes, Pete was quite unpleasant. We had fantastic sex. It was off the hook, all over the place, and very raw. And he was OK the next day. He was lovely. I remember feeling great when I left there. You see, I wasn't there to screw the stars. If it happened, it occurred. "When I met people like Pete Townshend, I thought, 'Wow, I guess I just slept with Pete Townshend!'"I started bodybuilding because I missed the lights. I began lifting and exercising, and the trainer at the gym said, 'Wow, you have excellent potential to be a bodybuilder'. He was correct, because I have the symmetry. So I started lifting and intended to compete before I was 40. I placed second in my first show! I did this for six years of my marriage. Tom's jobs required us to relocate frequently. My kid, Seamus, was born in Sacramento and has lived in San Diego, Florida, Texas, and now Seattle. Tom and I were together for 12 years. What occurred was that we began having three-ways. We were in San Diego, and Seamus was around eight. I told Tom, 'I guess I'm gay. He answered, 'No, you're not. I was crying and said, 'Yeah, I suppose I am'. He said, "I believe you, too, have a preference for ladies. I am willing to let you explore that side of yourself. So I met a woman and fell in love. Tammy was a huge bodybuilder with a stunning physique. I'd become sober in 1987 and hadn't had a drink in eleven years. Tammy introduced me to GHB, which marked the beginning of my demise. It dragged me down extremely far. It's a stimulant that targets the same dopamine receptors as alcohol, making you feel euphoric and giddy, as if you're the life of the party. It only lasts about an hour, after which you'll need another small dose or scoop. Tammy told me it would help with my bodybuilding, but I had stopped coming to AA and had forgotten I was a drug user. If you drink a little too much, you'll be there one minute and gone the next. Just out. I have a scar on my chin to show it. But it wasn't until I bought my first drink that I realised, "Wow." I am drinking. I haven't drunk in sixteen years. In April 2001, I checked into a women's treatment program in Seattle. I was their first GHB patient, and my withdrawals were really terrifying and acidic. I was lying in bed, resisting the moving ceiling. Then I thought, "You know what, Gayle? If this is what it is, just roll with it. While in therapy, I met a girl named Melody and had an affair. When I got out, I abandoned my marriage in a terrible way. He was still madly in love with us, expecting that the procedure would bring us back to life. Instead, I left with this woman and my son.

"At the age of 44, the only job I could find paid $12 per hour. Talk about humility. Mel and I broke up, and then I met my girlfriend Deb. And over time, as Tom worked on his program and I worked on mine, we got to a better place. I am currently the marketing director for a legal software company. Who would've guessed it? But I'm still on edge. Nobody would have suspected that I had spent fifteen years working in a law firm's library. I am a chameleon. I can play the part and put on the suit, but I can also go the opposite way. However, they respect my job, so I get away with it. I acquired my house one year ago. I am an avid Harley rider. I have a 2005 Softail Deluxe. I adore my bike. I'm glad I didn't bike before, since I would have probably ruined it. That is why God has not brought it into my life until now. So I bike with buddies, and life is great. And, guess what? I've been sober for five years today, April 11. I suppose some males will read this and remark, 'Thank God she quit drinking!' I'm going to the meeting tonight, where I checked myself into recovery, to receive my five-year coin. I have nice pals, and I'm healthy, which is a miracle. I adore what I do. Deb and I have broken up more than once, so what else is new? Welcome to the world of lesbian partnerships. She thinks it's horrifying that I'm conducting this interview, but I remember that time in my life as being full of wonderful events and so much fun! I have no regrets, but Deb believes you should sweep situations like mine under the rug. She adopts more of my mother's demeanour, and I respond, "Get over yourself!" It was fun! It's her problem, not mine. Being in recovery, I undoubtedly have codependency issues, which are all about letting go of your partner's difficulties. C'mon, that was twenty-five years ago, in another era.

"Many times I've sat in reflection, and I've realised that all of my drinking and drinking ruined what could have been a dream life with one of these people. I could have developed a number of those relationships further. I was definitely a hard person to be around at times. The Moody Blues video begins with a woman ironing in her home. She had obviously been a groupie, and she starts reflecting on her crazy past, asking, 'How did I get here?' And there were many years when I thought, 'Wow, my life is so uninteresting, look what it's come to. Now that I'm sober, I appreciate the memories, but when I buy a ticket to a performance, I don't want to be in the audience in my seat! I want to be up front, near, and feel a part of everything. About ten years ago, I attended an Aerosmith concert by myself. I was enjoying the show when this roadie offered me a pass and said, 'Come back after the show'. 'Oh my God,' I thought, 'I'm nearly forty years old and I still have it!'"

Chapter 10: Slow Dazzle

Margaret Moser, the queen bee of Austin's incredible music scene, requested me to speak on the first-ever groupie panel at the annual South by Southwest Music Conference a few years ago. It was one of the most well-attended panels of the year, and we had a great time educating the industry hipsters on the intricacies of groupiedom. Margaret and I got along like we'd known each other forever.

I've been enjoying Austin since that first groupie panel, and it's become one of my favourite places to visit. I've gained many friends, including Margaret's colourful younger brother, Stephen, who writes the Austin Chronicle's unfettered style column.

Margaret has been married twice before and is now happily in love with Burnin' Mike Vernon, guitarist for one of Austin's most renowned bands, 3 Balls of Fire. It's SXSW time again, and despite our insanely hectic schedules (seeing out hot bands), I manage to squeeze in a conversational hour alone with her over plates of spicy Mexican food. She is a senior staff writer for the Chronicle and has been in charge of producing the famous Austin Music Awards for over two decades. Last night, she inducted the cult band the 13th Floor Elevators into the Austin Hall of Fame.

Margaret informs me, dipping chips into fresh salsa, "I come from a literary background that encouraged reading of all kinds". "I am the one who reads the cereal box at the morning table. I read everything, including between the lines. Not only are people being written about, but also the writers themselves. I recall being in seventh school and looking at Janis Joplin's 45, 'Down On Me'. Powell St. John's song 'Bye-Bye Baby' appeared on the other side. I had no idea who it was, but the name stuck with me. I read music labels differently than other girls did. 'What exactly does producer mean? Who are the people on the liner notes? So inducting Powell St. John as a member of the Elevators—and remembering that Joplin label—was a full circle moment for me."

How did Margaret go from reading about music to being a part of it? "There weren't many options in San Antonio, and even kids who liked the Monkees didn't care who wrote the songs. Could the Neil Diamond who composed 'I'm a Believer' be the same Neil Diamond that my mother listens to? Are C. King and Goffin the same folks that wrote the girl-group records? I was connecting the dots, but I wasn't getting anywhere since I didn't have any kindred spirits. But when I picked up the Rolling Stone groupie issue, I thought, "Yeah, hey!" This is what I want to do! I didn't think groupies were sluts; they seemed like attractive, fun-loving young women to me. I felt like an outcast, so it was a chance for me to stand out and be my own person. I'd return to school after a show and think, 'Ha ha, you jackasses spent five bucks for a concert last night, and I was backstage'. My first encounter emulating GTOs was in 1971. I sewed baby-doll clothes for my girlfriends, with hands stitched over the breasts. I was working on my first written collection, 'The Groupie Papers', and I examined albums but didn't know how to get them published. I didn't have the same manly attitude as Cameron Crowe. So being a groupie was my entry point. I went in on my knees, eyes wide open."`

I'm always interested in learning how things began. "The first time I snuck backstage was for Joe Cocker's Mad Dogs and Englishmen. I merely sniffed around, and the insect bit me. Norman Mayell, Blue Cheer's drummer, was the first musician I slept with. The next thing I recall is a concert with Badfinger, Leon Russell, and Quicksilver. We were hanging around backstage, waving at the boys and allowing them to look at our dresses. I ended up sleeping with John Galley, who played keyboards with Leon Russell; I've always disliked keyboard and bass players. Then I was with Robert Cardwell of Mother Earth. He was my first encounter with cocaine and a massive dick, which amplified the entire situation. I'd arrive there about three p.m. for Jethro Tull or John Mayall's sound check, sneak my way backstage, and end up with someone!"

By spring 1976, Margaret had regained her freedom and was seeking her own creative expression. "I picked up the local underground newspaper and saw they were looking for someone to clean the office, and I thought, 'That's for me!'" I began cleaning up and answering phones at the Austin Sun, and the first thing I did was go around the music department. There was a new column titled Backstage. We were in a staff meeting when the editor said, 'What's going to be in Backstage this week? Nobody responded, so I replied,

"I know Randy California from Spirit." I can arrange an interview with him."

Margaret is still a regular at Austin's wonderful Driskill Hotel. Does she ever stroll past the restroom and remember that decadent night? "I was there in November with John Cale and was laughing my ass off. I was in that toilet with Mick Ronson for twenty minutes, having sex and snorting cocaine. After that, I went into one of the bedrooms and found Roger McGuinn. He was wearing a large belt buckle covered in rhinestones—it had to be the size of your tape recorder—and I was captivated by it. I was wearing one of those '70s gowns made of Nuestra, a glossy, clinging polyester that caught on everything. I glanced at Roger since I thought he was quite attractive. He was seated on the bed as I was standing up, and he grabbed me and began kissing my breasts. I said, 'You've been my hero since seventh grade,' and he said, 'How old were you in seventh grade?' I responded, 'Oh, eleven or twelve.' He said, 'Did you have to wear a school uniform?' I thought, 'Maybe he'd like me to wear anklets and black patent leather shoes as well'. I was absolutely engrossed, and the next thing I knew, we were in the restroom—yes, I know, sloppy seconds and all. My Nyestra dress had been ripped from the waist down. It was never worn again, but I saved it nonetheless."

I attempt to image bespectacled folkie Roger McGuinn battling it out atop the bathroom sink. "He was something else! I was loving it because he was all over me—unlike Mick Ronson, I knew who he was. "I walked around knock-kneed for the rest of the party."

Margaret claims she "embraced groupiedom" at that time. But she also had a budding literary career and made a crucial decision that night. "I wondered how I was going to compromise the pussy and the brain, both of which were going full tilt, so I decided not to sleep with local musicians anymore —that was where I drew the line" . Margaret laughs, "I just continued to sleep with national and touring musicians".

Margaret chose to attend an Armadillo gig by a former Velvet Underground member, based on the recommendation of a music-savvy acquaintance. "The instant I arrived backstage, I was pushed into the darkness, finding my way around, and ran into this guy wearing a hard hat and camouflage. He stared down at me, and I looked up to him. I gasped and could barely breathe. I didn't know who he was, but he led a lot of people onstage, and I simply went 'Uh, uh, uh...' The date was April 17, 1979. "I immediately fell in love with John Cale."

Margaret was intrigued by John's set, and she requested him to sign a poster she had pulled off the wall. "He grinned and asked my name. When I told him, he gave me a strange look and scribbled, 'Best wishes, Margaret'. I reached for the poster, but he yanked it back, forcing me to lean forward. He asked, 'What are you doing tonight?' I replied, 'Anything you want'."

Years ago, John Cale married one of the GTOs, Miss Cynderella, and I recently learned that the youngest member of our group died tragically. It's hard to imagine that there are just three Girls Together Outrageously remaining: Sparky, Mercy, and me. "We experienced our first Texas Blonde death four years ago, so I sympathise. It was heartbreaking," Margaret admits regretfully. "She was one of my best friends, and such a free spirit" .

Margaret formed her own kindred clan not long after her first dazzling experience with John Cale. "I had never forgotten the things I'd read about the GTOs. At the time, I was between newspapers and had recently split up with my photographer husband. It all started the night John played the Armadillo. That show literally took the top off of my skull, and all I wanted to do was listen to music. I was completely besotted. There was a thriving new wave culture, with bands such as the Romantics and Psychedelic Furs passing through town. I kept running across the same group of girls, so we started hanging out together. Then, in 1981, John was at the Armadillo again, and I discovered he was playing the Whisky in Los Angeles for three nights. I gathered the girlfriends, rented a car, and travelled to Hollywood. We booked a room at the Tropicana, where John was staying. I became good friends with his band, and they would come to our room after the show since we were the party girls, complete with drugs and booze. Their backup singer, Deerfrance, had a charming little girl voice, and one night she commented, 'You're all blonde and from Texas. You are the Texas Blondes'. I answered, 'Yes!' We arrived at the Whisky the next night, inebriated from being the Texas Blondes. Suddenly, we had an identity. And I knew exactly what we could accomplish with it because of the GTOs and Plaster Casters, who also served as role models for us. We were in the Whisky bathroom that night, wearing glittering eye shadow and applying bright red lipstick, when this dark-haired girl strolled in and asked, 'Who are you?' We looked at each other and smiled back at her, 'We're the Texas Blondes!" Saying it out loud confirmed it. We went to Los Angeles as a group of gals and returned back as Texas Blondes. We had Mexican and black girls over the years since it wasn't a matter of colour, but of mindset. And we became really well-known for it. Guys like having us in their arms. We were terrific eye candy and had a lot of fun."

A few months later, Margaret was thrown back to earth when John brought Reza, the girl he would marry, to Austin with him. "I was trying to be brave" , she said, "but my heart was bleeding all over the place" .

Margaret had recently married for the second time when she met John Cale again. "It was February 1985, and I hadn't seen him in five years. I remember it clearly since it was two months to the day after my wedding. Rollo, a tattoo artist, despised John Cale. John was married and had a baby. When he invited me to return to his hotel room, I thought, 'Oh my God, what am I gonna do?' This was the moment I'd hoped for for years. We kissed briefly, and I replied, "I just got married, and you have a wife." I can't do this. But I did stay out late with John that night, and when I returned home, there was hell to pay. When I got into the shower, Rollo assumed I was washing away my guilt, but I said, 'No, I didn't, I didn't, I didn't'. "Now I wish I had."

When John arrived in town, it was awkward for the following few years. "After that, he did not try again. I believe I injured his ego. But I'd see him anytime he came through, and I believe he figured I'd be here every time he visited Austin. He'd come to the airport seeking for someone to pick him up, and there I was. In 1988, I got him up and drove him to Driscoll. The doorman led us to the room, opened the door, and John entered. The doorman then held the door for me and said, 'Here you go, Mrs. Cake'. Just for a moment, I had the luxury of being Mrs. John Cale." Margaret sighed. "When I read John's biography, I discovered his mother's name was Margaret. Now

I understand why he gave me that look when I originally told him my name."

Margaret and Rollo were married for fourteen years, with the last few years spent in Hawaii. "I was so devoted that I suppressed my feelings for John and tried not to acknowledge them. Rollo defined everything I did, and when he became addicted to heroin, I felt isolated and deceived. I felt like a fish out of water surrounded by all that ocean, and I was eager to get back to Austin. It was 1993, and I hadn't been home long when I read Ann Powers' review of your second book in the New York Times, and you inspired me again from afar. Her post compared groupies to the Florence Nightingales of rock and roll, trading elegant bedside manners for blow jobs. I had sensed it all along, but I had never been able to express it. Here was another woman speaking for me. In addition, I am using my role model. I took it to SXSW and announced, 'There's a panel in this.'" Margaret has since been an active participant in the yearly convention, conducting panels and overseeing the stylish annual Austin Chronicle music awards.

I was a presenter again in 2006, and as I dashed off stage, Margaret presented me to Dayna, one of the Texas Blondes. "Dayna has worked with me the longest," Margaret tells me. "And in every case, it was what we learnt as groupies that let us work so successfully with bands. "We know all the tricks."

I ask Dayna for any unforgettable Texas Blonde stories. "I was with Iggy Pop for a while," she explains as she holds her clipboard. "He liked me from the beginning. Sweetheart that he was, he'd say, 'Aw, you're my little shithead; come here, darlin'. I was extremely young when he brought me on tour, and eventually his management said, "You cannot be dragging a fourteen-year-old girl across state lines." You are going to prison. I replied, "Well, I have to go back to school anyway." Shortly after, Iggy decided that he needed me to help him write. He arrived and remained with me, my mother, and father while I attended school. That lasted about a week, until my mother made him clean the dishes. Then he booked a hotel and I remained with him. Looking back, I say, 'What a paedophile!' I must have struck him as unusual. Sexually, I doubt I pleased him in the same way that a grown woman could. He has a gigantic cock—the size of your right arm—and I couldn't take it all the way because I was so young." Dayna swiftly returns after handing over an award to the next raucous presenter. "There was one person I stayed in touch with for years: Jerry Harrison of the Talking Heads. He was always there for me, and I loved him very much. We got together whenever he came to town, and when I relocated to New York, I lived with him. He's one of the most stand-up men I know. But they never treated me poorly. They gave me emotional strokes that I never received in high school, which helped me establish self-esteem later on. People say, 'Oh, poor thing, you were young and taken advantage of'. Yes and No. Logically, I can see it that way, but don't think I didn't gain anything from it! Margaret was well-known for her strength, and nobody fucked with me while I was under her wing. I followed where she went, and before you knew it, there were several of us. The publicists would bring in bands and ask, 'Can you get those blondes?' Suddenly, we emerged, and I realised, 'I'm in this great bunch that can travel anyplace. I met all the cool guys, and I can tell those individuals who thought I was a loser in junior high to kiss my ass!"

Marriage must suit Margaret Moser, as she is engaged again, this time to guitarist Mike Vernon. "One of my favourite posters of all time was for Three Balls of Fire. It was a photo of Mike playing guitar while wearing a large cowboy hat. He's lit from below in an eye-catching style, with flames on both sides of the instrument. It's quite powerful. Whenever they released a CD, I gave it uniformly positive reviews. I wrote a hilarious, foreshadowing one just four years ago: 'Mike Vernon plays with a lover's touch that leaves you breathless'. Who else will I fall in love with? I am weary of artistic pussies. I've dated physicians, lawyers, and married tattoo artists and photographers. I've been with both artists and non-artists, and I eventually fell in love with a politically conservative guitarist. A woman in her sixties told me, 'Conservative men make terrific husbands'. I'd never considered that. Mike's conservatism, however, is an important component of his dedication and desire to persevere. And I am totally willing to allow him to hold opposing opinions. "I'm not a flaming liberal, anyway." Her new boyfriend accepts Margaret's wild history and her long-standing fascination with John Cale. "The last time John was here, we had the most open, cordial connection we'd ever had with each other. It couldn't have been better, and Mike was content with it. Mike and I think similarly in a number of ways. Last week, we made one of our collaborative ideas come true. We gathered thirteen of the top guitarists in town to perform Link Wray's 'Rumble' live on stage. Mike came up with the idea for the Guitar Rumble, and we originally considered fifty guitars. We were driving down the street when I stated, 'Fifty guitars will never work'. I was thinking hard and finally came up with 'Thirteen Guitar Rumble', and he nearly drove off the road. He exclaimed, 'Oh, that's wonderful! We'd only been dating for ten days when he said, 'I'm going to marry you. I said, 'Okay, bud, you're on'."

Chapter 11: Flesh for Fantasy

Polly Parsons, my goddaughter, recently had her splashy evening wedding shower at a famed Moroccan restaurant on Sunset Boulevard, where clients happily delve into heaps of spicy cuisine with their bare hands. Polly's hungry guests were halfway through the tabbouleh and shawerma when intriguing, seductive music drifted through the mirrored curtains, drawing Princess Farhana to the centre of the room. I'd always recognized this colourful scenester as Miss Pleasant Gehman, the iconic punk/singer/writer/hipper-than-hip journalist, and here she was in yet another incarnation, wiggling and shimmying to beat the band while dressed in sheer, sequined, coin-laden odalisque clothing. Pleasant bared her curvaceous midriff and began her dervish whirls, banging her finger cymbals and captivating us one by one. Our jaws dropped as she did crazy belly rolls and suggestive bumps, her exuberant dark eyes flashing like desert moondust.

After another evening of her spectacular hip swaying, the lively, va-va-voom Pleasant invites me into a velvet-curtained hideaway and regales me with tales of her younger days. "I had a thing for the Beatles and the Rolling Stones. I grew up watching them on Ed Sullivan. I was enamoured with Ringo because of how he dressed. I thought George was the cutest, but whenever I had the chance, I'd get these rings from gumball machines and my brother and I would put them all on. My father yelled at him, 'You look like a homosexual!', which we misread as 'tag'. Obviously, if Ringo was a 'tag', it had to be a good thing. So we put on every fucking piece of jewelry we could find, and in the middle of this massive dinner party, we came downstairs and yelled, "Look everyone!" "We are tags!"

Pleasant bought a T. Rex album at the new neighbourhood mall after being "flabbergasted" by glitter-god Marc Bolan on TV; then she spotted David Bowie's Aladdin Sane. "That was the first time I shoplifted anything other than bubble gum, and I stole it just 'cause of the way the cover looked —then the next week I shoplifted Iggy's Raw Power, and those are still two of my favourite records on earth"
.

If you're going to take anything, make it worth it, right? When she took off a pair of white hot pants and wore them about the house, her mother was appalled. "Instead of asking where I acquired them, she responded, 'You look like Lolita'. I asked, 'Who's Lolita?' She instructed me to read the book, so I went up to our guest room and began reading. I evidently didn't hear her call us to supper because I was in there, stunned. I didn't think of Lolita as a paedophile; rather, I thought, "Wow!" Could a grown-up be that thrilled about someone my age? Woo-hoo!' I began to wonder about this power I possessed, and that same week I saw Cabaret, complete with all those outfits and the wild three-way. Forget that; I was never the same. When I discovered Bowie and Lou Reed, my life took a turn for the better. I knew what my path was. I aspired to be a truly glamorous creature— a 1930s cinema star crossed with a courtesan. Then I refined it to 'I wanna go to L.A., get high, and bang rock stars!' I spent the majority of my adolescence and twenties not thinking I was gorgeous, but when I look back at photos, I think, 'Oh my God, I could have conquered the world!'"

Pleasant and her friends soon began shoplifting clothes for rock concerts, concealing the fishnets, Lurex tube tops, and platforms beneath tie-dyed trousers and puffy Snorkel Arctic parkas. Their first covert adventure involved seeing Alice Cooper. "We stole everything we wore, including green nail polish, and stored all of our normal clothing in the Greyhound station locker. We put on lipstick, sparkles, and beauty marks before walking five blocks to the New Haven Coliseum in hot pants and tube tops, completely intoxicated and stoned. The guards wouldn't let us go backstage. Then I remembered reading in Rock Scene that Alice Cooper would always stay at Holiday Inns. I knew his manager's name and dialled the first Holiday Inn. 'Hello, may I have Shep Gordon's room, please? They immediately put me through, and I heard a huge party going on, so we hitchhiked over there. They let us party with them, but because we looked like fucking fetuses, nothing happened—even if we wanted it to."

Pleasant was sent to boarding school in Massachusetts for a variety of reasons, including illegal sex and drug addiction. "I received a full scholarship. My mother believed it would be good for me, but little did she know I was fucking out of control, having sex with everyone, and doing drugs, which was opening up new possibilities for me. Then mother informed me we were moving but didn't say where, and I cried for four hours because I finally had a group of people who didn't think I was insane."

She wasn't depressed for long because her mother had landed a position at 20th Century Fox in the City of Angels, a nirvana for any rock fan. "I assumed it was going to be Somewhere Horrifying, Iowa, and when she said, 'We're moving to Los Angeles,' I dropped the phone. I finished that term and travelled to Hollywood in the middle of my junior year. I had a first date with Rodney."

After sharing a welcome-to-Hollywood joint with "hot old man" Tony Curtis at a Tubes performance, she met a couple of future punk icons. "A few rows ahead of me, I noticed George and Paul, who subsequently became Pat Smear and Darby Crash. Georgie was dressed like Alice Cooper, while Paul wore all white with an Aladdin Sane lightning bolt and red hair. I threw them a note with my phone number: 'Aladdin Sane, you cosmic orgasm, call me'." Pleasant spent the next day slumming around the vibrant Hollywood Boulevard with her new friends. Two or three days later, they said, 'Do you like Iggy?' They knew where he lived and asked if I wanted to visit. Oh my God, yes! Are you kidding? 'Am I breathing?' So we caught the bus to Flores Street. I was so dumb that I assumed we were heading to a Jed and Granny Clampett Beverly Hillbillies-style house, but it was actually a 1920s flat. I thought he was in the penthouse, but no, he's in this terrible little, dark subterranean hovel up to your knees in clothes, fast food containers, beer bottles, open guitars with glasses full of cigarette butts on them, just misery."

Yes, it was a hellish hovel, but Pleasant was about to meet her first rock deity in person. "Iggy came out of the bathroom wearing small cutoff shorts with the fly open, and that was it. I was in awe because he looked so beautiful. His hair was all platinum, and he appeared tanned and robust. He was absolutely incomprehensible, but he had the most amazing figure, golden hair, and his name was Iggy POP!"

Pleasant knew she wanted to write about rock and roll from the day she arrived in Los Angeles, and when she graduated from high school in 1977, she did exactly that. "I adored Creem's writers. Lester Bangs was fantastic, but most of the content I encountered in local publications was dry and foolish. "I thought, 'I can write about music better than these people can'." She submitted samples and ended up working for numerous local publications, which helped her get to where she wanted to be: backstage. "I was at all those early underground punk shows and crazy parties at people's houses, so I decided to start my own magazine, having no idea how to do it". She dubbed the fanzine Lobotomy. "I imitated the Frederick's of Hollywood bag and added the phrase 'Where Glamour Is a Way of Life'. The first edition featured the Mumps on the cover. Lance Loud was the first person I ever interviewed, and he recognized it, saying, 'You're doing fantastic!'"

Pleasant wanted to stop for cigarettes, and when she entered the liquor store, she was astonished to see Iggy walk out. "He said, 'Let's ditch everyone and go see the dictators at the Whisky, come on!'" Iggy and Pleasant abandoned their dates, and she was soon smack dab in that gorgeous, incandescent image of glamour, zipping through the night in the large white convertible. The Whisky was full, so Iggy invited her to his Malibu home. "We were driving through the greenery of Beverly Hills, and he had his arm around me. He was extremely sweet, and I was ecstatic, but I felt a little weirded out that we had abandoned folks."

It got really cold travelling through Pacific Palisades, so Iggy bravely pulled over to manually yank up the top, fumbling with the numerous old-fashioned latches. "I was sitting there thinking, 'What should I do now?' Then he looks at me and says, 'I feel like Richie Cunningham in Happy Days'."Back at the pad, Iggy performed Pleasant demos of his new music. "Then he said, 'Let's go to sleep,' and we went to bed and had sex about seven times." That was insane! I had never been through anything like that before. I also had nothing to compare it to—at least not on that scale. I had been having sex, but I would go with someone and try a door on someone's good automobile; if it was open, we'd crawl into the back seat and have sex. Anyway, Iggy was completely fucking wonderful; he has a great figure, as everyone knows, and a tremendously big dick."

The next day, Iggy asked Pleasant if she wanted to live in for a bit. Because she still lived at home, she told him she'd commute back and forth. "The first time I stayed for three or four days, this guy named David was also living there, behaving like a houseboy. I'd be on the couch reading a book, and when I reached for a cigarette, David would be there with a lighter. One day, Iggy was utterly out of his mind, and David muttered, 'Oh, he's just painting. But I wasn't sure what that meant. Iggy was in this wild phase where he plastered the entire home with butcher paper and covered himself with gallons of house paint, acrylic paint, spray paint—all this shit—pouring it over himself, sprinting to the walls, and jumping against them. He was making full-body prints."

She was the younger of the two, yet Pleasant felt weirdly possessive of Iggy and was frequently disturbed that he was so spent. "I had a huge crush on him, and we were having amazing sex, but it was beyond my comprehension—the quantity of drugs he was using, running into walls, and so on. In many respects, I acted like his mother, but he was also protective of me; it was a warped form of home happiness."

At the conclusion of the summer, Iggy left Malibu to record with Bowie and explore the depths of Berlin. He promised to remain in touch, but Pleasant didn't expect him to follow through. She didn't give up when he didn't call. "It went on and off throughout the summer and was quite interesting and cool. But I had no concerns about the future—in fact, I couldn't believe anything had happened at all. There was no perspective to put the entire event into. I felt a little lucky. I wouldn't call it a blessing, but I considered it a privilege.

When Pleasant returned to Los Angeles, she fell for Levi Dexter and the Rockats' wild rockabilly attractions. "The Rockats were all adorable. They resembled horror films in a terrific way. They had all these fashion models draped about them, and Marianne Faithfull was sniffing around. They were the It Boys, transforming the punk culture into rockabilly." Pleasant wanted to stand out from the punked-out, green-haired leather crowd, so a photo shoot with the Rockats and the gals that hung out at the Masque was planned. "I thought, 'I need to appear like Sophia Loren or Gina Lollobrigida'. I painted my nails and applied movie star makeup. Instead of spiking and greasing my hair, I let it be soft. I wore a bias-cut zigzag '50s top with high heels and the tightest pencil skirt I could find. I stepped in wearing my bullet bra, and the photographer said, 'Why don't you stand right between those two?' referring to Levi and Smut. It worked like a charm!"

I remember when the blazing punkabilly Rockats rolled into town with their Brit Teddy-Boy sneers and radical rockabilly pomps, aided by Miss Mercy's terrifying scissors. All the females grovelled for Levi, but Pleasant's obvious charms won him over, and they became a popular item. When Levi was on tour, Pleasant proceeded down the same rough path, mad about a stunning British up-and-comer, Billy Idol, the lead singer of Generation X. She wrote great reviews for Lobotomy and immediately sent them to his record label in London, along with spray-painted Gen-X T-shirts and a bluntly open love letter.

Fortunately, her old buddy Rodney Bingenheimer was quickly becoming the hipster DJ at KROQ, and he invited her to the studio the night Billy called in from England. "So I'm hyperventilating, and Rodney says, 'OK, someone wants to talk to you'. I say, 'Hello, this is Pleasant', and Billy says, 'Oh, I got your package last week'. "We were on the phone for an hour and a half."

A few weeks later, Billy arrived in town and had no trouble finding Pleasant. Another would-be groupie pursued them around the market, attempting to horn in while they were purchasing vodka, but Pleasant did what any self-respecting cat eyed doll would do: she let the air out of her tires. She took Billy up to Runyon Canyon for a stunning view of Los Angeles. "I thought it would be a really cool site to take him since it had a fantastic pirate, jungle vibe, tons of L.A. history, and you could see the entire city. We had already smoked marijuana, and one hit of marijuana is equivalent to three pills of acid for me. We were looking at the vista and said, 'Fuck, it's magnificent.'"

So, what was it like to look at Billy Idol in the moonlight? "He was one of the most attractive people ever. His skin was like cream. No shit, he looked like he was carved from jewels. He had white hair and resembled a newborn chick in a good guy way. He had amazing eyes and was really witty. He had a quick wit, a hilarious laugh, and a keen sense of humour. Maybe he wasn't the most cerebral person on the planet, but he was quick, well-read, perceptive, and caustic without being nasty. He had an interesting distorted perspective on things. He could have been a gigantic jerk, but he was not."

Pleasant took Billy to a big party the next day, and the market's pushy groupie returned and refused to leave. "She was being completely uncool, and I was no stranger to brawls and bar fights. Joan Jett was present and said, 'I got your back' since it appeared that there would be a large girl fight. I don't think I intended to light her hair on fire, and I wouldn't do it today, but it seemed like a nice idea at the moment. So I lightened up a large section of her hair with a lighter." Pleasant measures around three inches with her fingers, smiling sheepishly, "Like about that much".

To earn funds to publish Lobotomy, my great friend Michele Myer, who booked the Whisky, proposed that Pleasant perform benefit concerts. On one of these nights, Billy was the guest of honour.

"It was just our buddies helping out, but the bills were outrageous—the Go-Gos, the Weirdos, and the Germs. Joan Jett lived across the street, so anytime we went to the Whisky, particularly on Lobotomy evenings, we'd prime the pump at her house. Gil Turner's Liquor served alcohol even though no one was above the age of 21, since we'd answer the door in black underwear, handcuff belts, and high heels. We'd start the order with a gallon of vodka and then blitz. Billy came over to Joan's that night, and we completely outdid ourselves. We had Nancy bound to the bed with socks, linens, and clotheslines. There were three to four different types of whips. We were all on Quaaludes, and the Sex Pistols were firing. The front door was open, and the coffee table was covered in beer bottles. We heard screams and Michele Myer rushed into Joan's apartment from the Whisky, so the show must have been very late. She noticed all the beer bottles, the trail of garments, and Nancy spread eagle on the bed. Billy was clutching a gallon of vodka and a cat o' nine tails while swinging. She cries, "You—the show producer—get to the fucking Whisky." You—the stage manager—get to the fucking whiskey. She screams at Billy, "And you—the fucking guest of honor..." while shaking her finger. And he adds, 'Sorry, madam'."While Pleasant romped with Billy Idol, Levi Dexter was conveniently on tour. "Oh, he was in England banging someone else, or he may have been in New York at that time with Belinda from the

Go-Gos. I told her to fuck him so he wouldn't fuck another foolish female. I mean, we completely flipped, and I took care of her lover, Bill Bateman from the Blasters. This was how you kept people loyal in the 1980s, right? Let them fuck your best friend. I believe Jane also fucked Levi, but in the late '70s/early '80s, courtesy of Quaaludes and cocaine. It was like unrestricted love in leather. It was no big deal that we had boyfriends and crushes together. It was simply a ridiculous pass-around. I had sex with or made out with the majority of the girls I knew, including Belinda and Jane. I actually had a brief affair with Jane, which began one night when we locked ourselves in a bedroom at someone's parents' house. While Levi and the Rockats were jamming with the Rockabilly Rebels, Jane and I had a long make-out lesbo session that lasted quite some time."

The Dexters moved into a cockroach- and pop-star-infested apartment building that Pleasant dubbed "Disgraceland". Unfortunately, the powder blue wedding turned out to be the highlight of the difficult two-year punkified marriage.

"As soon as we married, he began domestic violence. He would wake me up by striking me. He stayed home and smoked cannabis. all day as I rode a forty-five-minute bus to Century City with a massive hangover to work as a secretary wearing clothing borrowed from my mother. Finally, I said, "You need to get up." He gave me a black eye and threw me against a concrete wall, attempting to remove a tattoo I had recently received. "I said, 'Get out of my fucking house!' but he refused." Pleasant dashed off with a beautiful skateboard champion and had a ragingly wild fling in San Francisco to ensure Levi's departure. "When I returned, Levi asked, 'Were you fucking him?' I replied, "Yeah, of course—that was the whole point!" We're done. You need to get out. "And he finally realised it."

Pleasant fulfilled a long-held dream by fronting the Screamin' Sirens, followed by the Ringling Sisters, in the mid-1980s. "I decided I wanted to sing because I had been writing poems and songs since high school." I could mimic every guitar solo, but I never learned how to play. But because everyone said I was flashy and extroverted, I said, 'OK, I'll sing'. I sucked at first. I have a girlie Phil Spector voice, which is popular right now. But in those days, you had to be a punk screamer or a singer like Aretha Franklin. I wanted the band to be entirely female since it was working so well for my friends, the Runaways and the Go-Go's. I thought, 'I'm going to form an all-girl gang band that will be a cross between Old West saloon girls and bikers. "And we're going to play country music!" The band toured extensively, and Pleasant not only delighted people with her trilling, but also threw her full body into the mix. "Through the whole set I was dancing and shaking, nonstop for forty-five minutes' '.The foresightful girl who sensed Pleasant's inner sultan teaser was a belly dancer herself. "I began stalking her at parties." Everyone assumed we were trapped in the bedroom doing drugs, but she would show me hip figure eights. "People would bang on the door, 'Can I have some?'"

I ask Pleasant if she believes belly dancing is her "calling," already knowing the answer because I've seen her perform. "Completely! I could do it right away, and I resembled a belly dancer—I have dark eyes and a curved figure. I started dancing for fun at the age of 32, and within six months, people were paying me and exclaiming, 'You're the best belly dancer I've ever seen!' I always smiled when I danced. I've been doing it for fourteen years now, and I'm forty-six. Who starts a dance career at the age of 32?"

In 1997, Pleasant's writing assignment brought an ageing fair-haired boy into her office: she interviewed Iggy Pop for Request magazine. They were discussing a literary project Iggy was thinking about when things got amorous.

"I'm being Miss Professional, and since I had two novels out, he asked me about publishers. He planned to write a book titled 52 Girls since there are 52 weeks in a year and 52 cards in a deck. He suddenly starts kissing me. And we kissed for quite a while." Iggy wanted to take Pleasant to see Metallica that night, but she declined because she needed to work. Iggy was shocked to learn that Pleasant was a belly dancer. "'Arabic music has so much soul'," he stated. 'It's full of passion. "I want to come see you!"

Pleasant omitted to inform Iggy about the very rigorous dress code, so he arrived in a full torn Iggy costume. "I heard this commotion at the door but didn't see what it was because we were in the middle of a number" . Pleasant, balancing a sword on her head, noticed Iggy's platinum hair. "He was the only one with white hair in the entire place. Later, the troupe leader yells, "Oh my fucking God, Pleasant." What's Iggy Pop doing here? I know this must be your fault!"

Even though she was quaking inside, Pleasant must have delighted Sir Jagger, because he smiled, his dimples on full display, and gently tipped her a hundred dollars. She admits to storing the bill for six months until she "was pretty sure the DNA had worn off".

Pleasant Gehman, nicknamed Princess Farhana, the "Flower of the Desert," is at the pinnacle of her profession, captivating audiences with her dancing practically every night of the week. She is currently happy in a long-term relationship with James Packard, a skilled artist. Pleasant is enraged when I add that groupie, despite its seven letters, is still considered a four-letter word as we walk back to our automobiles in the blazing sunbeams of Southern California.

"I've always been fascinated by folks who work behind the scenes, and groupies were the most gorgeous. I connected them to artists' models from the 1920s since I was familiar with Man Ray and his muse, Kiki. Groupies served as a complement to rock stars. When they entered the room, everyone gasped. They were gorgeous, intelligent, and capable of handling any scenario. They were the epitome of a courtesan in the seventeenth century: clever, well-spoken, worldly women who were revered—and just let everyone eat cake. My mother asked, "Why do you want to be a groupie and not a star?" A groupie is a star! There were groupies who were movie and music stars. Marianne Faithfull was a groupie. Pat Smear was a Queen groupie, Darby Crash was a boy groupie, and both became stars. Angie Bowie was equally important as David Bowie. She had songs composed about her. Angie's art was just to exist. Her husband penned wonderful tunes, but Angie was the belle of the ball. That is a big talent in and of itself. Being a groupie does not imply that you are involved in shady activities backstage. "Being a groupie is like being the high priestess of rock and roll."

Chapter 12: A Chat Regarding the Infamous G Word

There have been only a few groupie books released by the muses of rock. I believe the first was Jenny Fabian's Groupie, released in 1969, which lightly disguises her flings with Pink Floyd, the Nice, and the Animals throughout London. Angela Bowie delivered tales about the Thin White Duke with caustic gusto in Backstage Passes in 1993, while the same year, the late Cyrinda Foxe-Tyler alternately savaged and admired her rock husband in Dream On: Livin' on the Edge with Steven Tyler and Aerosmith. Marianne Faithfull fearlessly demonstrated how low she could go while being the coolest lady to ever hold a cigarette or a Stone in 1994's Faithfull. Cynthia Plaster Caster is currently working on her fantastic art-cum-sex memoir, Catherine James has recently sold her biography to St. Martin's Press, and my own raucous contribution, I'm with the Band, has been reissued and is selling well, I'm pleased to report.

Bebe Buell's Rebel Heart, published in 2001, was the most recent new groupie tome. Our works are regularly mentioned in the same breath, and if you check at Amazon's entry for Band, you may see a recommendation to buy Rebel Heart as well. After all, the universe of groupies is small!

Bebe has had troubles with the G word for years, so I thought it was fitting to share her well-informed perspective on the subject.

Pamela: I would like to ask you a few questions about the term "groupie". I understand you prefer "muse".

Bebe: However, saying such leads to misunderstanding. Because using the word muse to describe yourself seems narcissistic. However, I believe it is OK to note the distinction.

Pamela: It all depends on who uses the word.

Bebe: I suppose if Picasso stated, "She's my muse," it would have a far bigger impact. Perhaps one of his many mistresses, whose initials he had to conceal in his paintings so he could honour her without informing his wife. If she declared, "I was the muse for that painting," society would immediately reject her.

Pamela: However, you have publicly said that you favour that word over the G word.

Bebe: Muse is a far more wonderful term. It simply sounds prettier. It's much more romantic. I am going to read you something I wrote. It's only one paragraph long, yet it pretty much summarises everything.

"As for the groupie tag, I don't think it signifies the same thing today as it did in the 1960s and 1970s. The term groupie, like other misused phrases such as punk and grunge, is now used to describe nearly anyone involved with musicians. As a result, I no longer identify with the term. The innocence that formerly accompanied the phrase has been replaced by an almost "anything goes" attitude. I'm sure it's an insult to females like Pamela Des Barres, Cynthia Plaster Caster, and the GTOs—who popularised the term—to be grouped in with women who sleep with anyone linked with a band or crew. In the traditional definition, a groupie is not like that... The music was, and still is, the most essential thing to a true groupie of the past; I find the modern definition of the term demeaning and inaccurate. It helps me get back up."

Pamela: I believe many people see the word as a slur.

Bebe: Or a mud wrestler high on drugs!

Pamela: But I met these gals known as the Beatles BandAides and the Rock N' Dolls. They go around in groups, claiming the word again.

Bebe: If they can clean it up and persuade people to appreciate true art again, I'd be thrilled. I'm sick and tired of seeing it associated with scantily clad chicks with no brows and plastic breasts.

Pamela: I first heard the word around 1968, and it wasn't derogatory. It was only a word.

Bebe: That was cool! I recall seeing you in Rolling Stone when I was in high school. The images appeared quite glamorous. You did not look at them and say, "Eeewww, those whores!" It was very rock & roll. There was also the necessity of becoming "eye candy". However, girls can offer a social scene to a band. You brought them shopping and introduced them to influential people, much as

Marianne Faithfull introduced Mick Jagger to English society. There was an air surrounding what girls like you did. And then it turned a little crazy.

Pamela: I'm very friendly with Lori Mattix now, but it happened right around the early '70s, when the newborn girls started wearing those tiny little hot pants...

Bebe revealed that they began having sex at the age of fourteen. That seemed strange to me because I hadn't had sex till the age of eighteen.

Pamela: Yes, I was 19.

Bebe: We were definitely prehistoric! I can't imagine having sex at fourteen.

Pamela: I had my Barbie dolls arranged in a row.

Bebe: Going out with Todd [Rundgren] exposed me to the entire culture pretty rapidly. Of course, if you get to live the rock and roll lifestyle, that's fantastic.

Pamela: My buddy, Cassandra Peterson (Elvira), was a huge groupie! She likes what she has done and proudly claims it.

Bebe: I heard she and Todd had a [conspiratorial mumble] "sexual romp". I believe it's fantastic. Everybody should fuck Todd.

Pamela stated that when she was backstage, the term "groupie" was similar to "roadie" or "road manager". She would boldly announce, "I'm a groupie," and people would exclaim, "Oooooooooh...".

Bebe: I'm not upset with the actual word. I would be an idiot if I said I had never hung out with a rock band, dated or married a rock star, or seen a lot of music in my life. Because it is a part of my identity. But I'm not going to allow anyone to label me stupid or judgmental because of it. What is the equivalent today? "I'm a stripper!" . "I'm a porn star!" . Aaahhh! Everyone's a little bit of a groupie regardless. We are all fans of something. The musicians do not receive any credit for choosing us and wanting to be with us. Doesn't that imply we have to be pretty very fucking exceptional and intelligent? That we weren't throwaways, one-night stands, or discards? We were the girls they sought out and wanted to be around, and they needed our energy. Everyone in the crowd who appreciates a band should compliment the females backstage! The genuine heart and soul of a moving concert is similar to an organism. Certain flowers won't grow unless their shit is in place.

Pamela: You're stating virtually exactly what Lexa Vonn from the Plastics said. She's a huge Marilyn Manson fan.

Bebe: I can see why someone would be liking Marilyn Manson. He's easily one of my favourite rock stars.

Pamela believes that Manson showed her that art is more than simply a song or a painting. "Art is the essence of who you are."

Bebe: That is quite fantastic. We live in a society in which half of the population considers it a cool term, linked with a glamorous and innocent era in rock culture. Some people equate it with sluts, blowjobs, and roadies.

Pamela: That is why I am writing this book. I'm going to get some serious shit for it.

Bebe: Polish up your skin right now, girl! My book came out five years ago, and I'm discovering that it's split down the middle. People either love it or dislike it completely. And I think that's fantastic. I am going to cite Marilyn Manson because I believe he is a genius! He claimed that all of the best art is either adored or hated—there is no in-between. That has proven to be true for me. So I am pleased.

Pamela: Lexa also stated that she believes music emanates from God or whatever higher power source exists. Musicians channel that source, and when they gaze at you with those eyes, it seems like you're with God."

Bebe: That is very well expressed. It practically has George Sand's ring. It sounds like she's referring to Liszt or Chopin. I fully agree with her. If you don't see that, you're not a groupie.

Pamela: It's so unfortunate how soiled the word has become.

Bebe: I was browsing industry forums, including the Velvet Rope, when someone created this discussion titled "Groupies, Groupies, Groupies". I purposefully did not publish, but I did watch it. This is another perspective on the word, which is why I despise it right now.

And, God bless her, she may adore animals and have a lovely garden, but Miss Connie doesn't help matters either.

Pamela: But she's the real deal, and she enjoys the music.

Bebe: She has had a song written about her, and she has never hurt anyone, that is for sure. I need to read this last post to you. Someone writes, "I imagine that being a rock star's sperm receptacle is not a good professional decision. "Groupies, take note." See? This is how some people see things.

Pamela: Unfortunately, yeah, and most of those folks are jealous in some way.

Bebe: That is feasible. But take note that the girls who are considered the crème de la crème of the groupie crop—every single one of them, including you—have had careers. Pattie Boyd and Jane Asher, like me, have careers. They contain substance. There's a reason these guys wished to be with Linda McCartney or Patti D'Arbanville. They are powerful, gorgeous, independent ladies who are well-connected and make their guys seem great!

Pamela: Yes, it appears that even goofy-looking musicians attract the beautiful girls.

Bebe: Power is aphrodisiac. There's something quite appealing about a normal, geeky guy strapping on a guitar and becoming Roy Orbison. I've always admired men like Arthur Miller, so it's no wonder that I'm drawn to intelligent guys like Rick Nielsen, Elvis Costello, and Todd Rundgren. In his own way, Stiv Bators was a brilliant being. Physically, he was unique. It was also quite exciting to date an alien, you know? He was one of the best boyfriends I've had. And I miss him.

Pamela: You don't have any regrets, right?

Bebe: I can't say that totally, because I obviously do. When I was younger, I did a lot of silly things that I would not do now. I would have preferred more children, therefore I do have some regrets. It's not like I didn't have any chances. But now that I have a grandchild, I get to experience that relationship. It's an incredible feeling to hug my daughter in my arms while she holds her baby. I cannot tell you how overwhelming that is.

Pamela: I'm glad for you. So, I assume that was all worthwhile?

Bebe: Yes. I recall going backstage at a Cheap Trick gig and seeing Rick Nielsen's face light up. It is a beautiful thing. They look at you and say, "Oh my God, you're here!" We're going to play so fucking awesome tonight!" They want to know that their females are present. And when they leave the stage, we'll give them the truth: "You sucked," "You were brilliant," "The bass player overplayed," or "It was horribly mixed." We know our crap! There were only a few It Girls who were treated like rock stars and retained their position.

Pamela: And it's still happening in dressing rooms and tour buses around the world.

Bebe: Yes, but you should strive to educate people. Feminism is not a terrible thing when properly explained. But Gloria Steinem had to continue fighting, saying, "Listen, this is what I mean. This is what I am trying to tell you. "Women can do anything." Either we have to reclaim the term "groupie," invent a new one, or educate people about what it actually means.

Pamela: That is what I hope to do.

Chapter 13: Come as You Are

I have always been captivated with rebellious people, from Mozart to Walt Whitman, Elvis to Eminem. I admire them for not being able to keep their candour, rage, and bare truth hidden, even when it hurts like hell.

So, where have all of the offended rock stars gone? Real rock stars are expected to overturn tables, point fingers, and shake drumsticks against the weak, devious status quo. I believe Kurt Cobain was the last rock star to cause such mayhem in the world. Like Dylan, he was able to express what was on his disillusioned followers' thoughts. For better or worse, he single-handedly changed rock fashion forever, yet his musical and societal contributions far outweighed the myriad of flannel-wearing wannabes who whined and mourned in his wake. He was a multitalented, severely angst-ridden genius who exposed small-minded hypocrisy and the shameless selling of his pissed off generation. Nirvana altered music in the same way that the Sex Pistols did a decade before, and it was a welcome slap in the face. Kurt unknowingly drew alarmingly near to what he was raging against, which I believe contributed to his decision to leave us all behind. I met him once when I interviewed Courtney Love at their unkempt home in damp, dreary Seattle, and his anguish dominated the room.

In my search for open-hearted groupies, Lexa from the Plastics suggested I meet a seductive, edgy brunette who has made a name for herself as a Hollywood singer. "Miss B," as she prefers to be referred to in this chapter, also spent numerous nights with Kurt Cobain when he donned his rusty grunge crown.

She makes no apologies for the harsh and murky turns her life has taken, but she is feeling more positive these days. She had emailed me some stunning images of herself—heavily darkened, come-hither brown eyes, extra low cut black lace accentuating her sumptuous curves—so I was shocked by her first reticence when I arrived for our interview. She has just moved into a gorgeous deco apartment in West Hollywood, and the only item on the walls is a poster for Gus Van Sant's film Last Days, in which Michael Pitt plays Kurt Cobain to perfection. Miss B's attention is drawn to three adorable baby kittens who alternately purr in our laps as we talk.

Today Miss B is a member of two local rock bands: Krell, a metal band she describes as "Marilyn Manson meets Black Sabbath," and a tribute cover band that primarily performs Jefferson Airplane songs. She has been writing for local Hollywood newspapers for ten years. She played a minor recurring part on HBO's Deadwood. She also admits to being a longtime groupie, but wishes the term hadn't become so stigmatised. "I've had people call me 'Oh, you're such a groupie,' and I laugh and say, 'You wish you were!' Sid and Nancy, Kurt and Courtney, are two rock stars who marry their groupies. What is a groupie, anyway? Someone who likes music and wants to be around it. I dislike it when it is used in a pejorative manner since everyone wants to get backstage. I went to a show recently, and my friend wondered, 'How do we get back there?' I said, 'I'll be back'. I just came in, and she despised me for it. I said, 'Sorry, but I'm good at this'. I'd also like to note that, from a musician's perspective, most band members are also groupies because they enjoy being around other groups. You might argue that roughly half of the world is made up of groupies, right?"

I couldn't agree more.

Miss B's late teens and early twenties were turbulent and dangerous, and she readily confesses she never imagined she'd make it to thirty, a watershed point she reached five years ago. "I wanted to lead the perfect rock 'n' roll lifestyle. When I was eighteen or nineteen years old, the difficult stuff started. I'm not sure if I planned it that way, but I was living the life and was around it all the time."

Miss B quickly connected with a variety of hard rockers when hanging around on the Vegas Strip in the mid-1980s. "There have been quite a few," she says openly. "I was with several guys from Pretty Boy Floyd, Jeff Pilson from Dokken, and I had a brief sexual contact with Lemmy from Motörhead. He's a strange one. "He's probably the oldest guy I've ever been with; he's been around since Jimi Hendrix days."

Miss B may have been crazy, but she clearly does not enjoy kinkiness or group sex. "I'm not the type of groupie that wrecks people's homes. I was proud that I had not stolen anyone's lover. I've never had threesomes or more than twosomes in my life. I've seen some things happen with other individuals but never participated. The only rock musicians I knew who were into truly insane stuff were Guns N' Roses, and I saw them having orgies. I was at Slash's place once with Duff, and I saw Slash and Ron Jeremy in bed with some porn actors. But I don't bother with it. I'm not into the whole business." She did, however, share the sack a few times with their mysterious frontman, Axl Rose. "Axl was more of a friend who evolved into, like, a lover. He was sensual and really nice. He's an intriguing individual, but he's shorter than the type of guy I generally choose. That was his dilemma: he was really short but wanting to be all masculine. I believe Axl suffered from short-man syndrome, which caused him to overwhelm others. I suppose it's partly because he grew up on a farm in Indiana with a terrible stepfather who abused him. He's withdrawn and prefers to smoke weed and drink than use drugs."

I saw GNR open for the Stones in the thick of their rock peak and was captivated by Axl whooping it up, slip-sliding back and forth in his bicycle shorts and tossing his long, fiery hair in every direction. Unfortunately, I've heard that Axl is a bad-tempered scalawag who frequently beats up his wife and girlfriend. "He did not lash out at me because I did not give him an opportunity. I know he's done terrible things to women, but I never became linked to him in that manner. Besides, he is doing well now. We were more like pals and did not sleep together very much. Even when we had sex, there were so many people in the other room. He understood about my past, therefore he was very gentle with me. Contrary to popular assumption, every time I was with him, he tried to calm me down. Normally, he flips out on others, but I was freaking out, and he was kind, saying, 'C'mon, calm down!' I'll always consider him a buddy.

Since I know Miss B is still friendly with Axl, I ask if she has heard Chinese Democracy, the infamous record he worked on for over eight years.

"He was going to use my voice on one of the tracks, but they never released the record. It's techno, and record labels didn't believe in it.

It's like Ozzy suddenly switched to techno because Axl was such a metalhead."

So, what happened? Why did he suddenly change his music and himself so dramatically with techno beats and bizarre braided hair extensions? He now appears to be impersonating Axl Rose in his heyday. "I know he's had a lot of surgery," Miss B explains. "He wants to look younger again. I suppose he's attempting to look like a hip-hop artist, but it's not working." Like many reclusive musicians, Axl appears to have lost contact. "Oh, he is obviously a hermit. Whatever he does, he does with the few people around him. He lives in Malibu with a South American maid who is very protective of Axl." Unfortunately, Axl's life sounds like a rock and roll Sunset Boulevard, with Axl Rose playing Norma Desmond. "Yeah" , stated Miss B, "except that his housekeeper looks like a tattooed Barbie from Brazil" .

Miss B was gradually drawn into Hollywood's sad but growing hard drug scene in the late 1980s. She was spending a lot of time with heroin addicts, and a quiet, skinny blonde from Seattle quickly became her daily copping partner. "I used to hang out with a lot of individuals who took that type of narcotic, and Kurt Cobain and I met in those circles. He became a friend. I was always a friendly person, and people liked me. It began with him providing me rides and taking me to acquire narcotics. I remember him complimenting me a lot—I hadn't had much of that growing up, so I really appreciated that about him."

There was an underground excitement about Nirvana's debut album, Bleach, which was already a pre-grunge masterpiece, and they were performing in small venues around town. Miss B claims that, surprise, Kurt's desire was to relocate his band to sunny California. "He wanted to get away from the Seattle situation. Despite his fondness for Washington, he aspired to make it in California. I believe being up in Aberdeen contributed to his sadness because he carried that bleak attitude with him—it did not improve when he moved to Los Angeles. Still, he wanted to live the California dream; he was going to compose music, and he wanted to do so here. He was quite intelligent. He was well-read and philosophical, but the drugs undoubtedly distracted him."

These "certain" errands were primarily unlawful, but spending so much time together fostered affection between the two young misfits. "He was a great sweetheart; he was a little slender but handsome, small-boned, and not as tall as I prefer, but he was hot. A large part of our relationship revolved around going to obtain dope, returning, and doing it. We simply became friendly in that way. Kurt and I both struggled with low self-esteem. He was without a doubt the most kindhearted rock star I'd ever met. It's funny because we were both the same way. I'm not sure who was the more outgoing of the two—probably myself, given how shy he was. I never understood why, but he suffered from the same affliction as I did: self-loathing. I can't say I feel that way anymore because I enjoy myself. But I still have the terrifying opposite side that Kurt had all over. He didn't feel deserving of anything, you know? That is why I believe he struggled with fame. It was overwhelming, and he did not feel deserving of it, which is quite unfortunate."

I agree that Kurt appeared to be the most clearly pained artist since Vincent Van Gogh severed his earlobe and sent it to a hooker. "He was nearly Gothic. If he had black hair, he would have been a Goth. "He was in a lot of trouble and was in constant pain," Miss B continues. "He had stomach problems—bleeding ulcers—and would become really unwell. However, his complaints were not limited to bodily issues. "He was in mental pain."

I understand that Kurt's heroin use must have alleviated some of his agony, but didn't Miss B worry that he would die inadvertently from an overdose?

"Yes," she responds slowly, "and he was always tragic, as were most of the men I've been with. According to what I've heard, Jim Morrison was also like that. They all share a common theme: a kind of death wish. So I understood from the beginning that things may go wrong. He was a suicidal person—if you knew him, you'd know. Most people in rock 'n' roll have it to some extent. They're not like the rest of us; they're a distinct breed."

I see that Kurt's need to express himself triumphed over his suffering long enough for him to make some of the most profoundly impactful music in rock history.

"Yeah, well, most artists, actors, or musicians, a lot of them are shy people but they come out of their shells during their music and their acting".

Somewhere along the way, the kindred wounded souls began spending evenings together. "I don't even know how it happened, but it did, and Kurt was an excellent, tender lover," Miss B sighs profoundly before revealing some fairly powerful information about Kurt Cobain. "Basically, he was into cross-dressing".

I ask Miss B where Kurt obtained the various women' outfits. "He had some of his own women's clothes made for him", she recounts. "And he was the type of person who would enter your closet. He was also a dumpster diver, and he recovered items from the trash. I can vouch to this because I witnessed it firsthand. He would pick random locations throughout Hollywood and then bring a package of women's clothes to my house, along with wigs, makeup, and jewellery. I'm not sure where he acquired the wigs. He would also wear my belongings. I used to be glam, obsessed with cosmetics and fashion. I was stylish—perhaps more so than I am today. I had Lip Service skull and crossbone jeans, everything amazing, and Kurt was really creative with the clothing."

Miss B relocated to Florida around the time Kurt returned to Seattle. "I was barely twenty years old, and I left Los Angeles to avoid being destroyed. I was so deep into the scene and so messed up on drugs."

When Miss B returned from her healing trip to Florida, she met Eddie Vedder of Pearl Jam, another Seattle favourite. They ended up at the iconic Riot House for a night of partying. Mr. Vedder has always appeared low-key and impenetrable. How did she make that happen? "I went backstage at his concert and met him," she states simply. "I have a knack. I just do it—I can't explain how I do it. I ended up knowing a lot of people, and I sort of worked it. It was probably due to the way I was dressed: very provocative with my boobs out, tight T-shirts, and Lip Service slacks. But I was still grimy. I worked on my sexiness. I once attended the Billboard Awards and interviewed George Harrison, which is something few people can claim. I really capitalised on the fact that I wrote for a rock magazine. I took full use of my youth and beauty. Yeah, I had a fantastic time with Eddie, but his demeanour was less engaging than Kurt's."

Soon after her close experience with Pearl Jam's sensitive wailer, Miss B met a roadie for Slayer, fell in love, and settled into an eight-year rock romance that was rather normal. They even made it legal, but she soon realised that marital happiness was not what she had dreamed for. "My marriage ended, but we remained excellent friends. I went right back to my old rockstar regimen. I reconnected with Time and resumed my old practices. I ended up loving Taime a lot. I wanted to be his girlfriend. According to what I've heard, Taime Downe cannot be tamed or tied down. Miss B objects, "Oh, I think he could be". "He has long-term girlfriends. But I pressed the subject. I had a crush on him and called him constantly. "I could have done the same thing with Kurt if he had been around longer."

What is it about Time that makes Miss B feel so passionate? "I think he's had an incredible impact on the Los Angeles scene. He's accomplished a lot musically. Taime is a fantastic frontman, and I believe he will go down in history—not like Nirvana, of course, but his band, Faster Pussycat, has a large cult following. I adore his rendition of 'You're So Vain' and the cover of 'These Boots Are Made for Walkin'. And he has a lot of excellent original material."

I interrupted Taime's tirade by asking Miss B what she'd been listening to lately except Taime Downe. "I currently listen to gothic music, metal, and vintage rock. I aim to have a mixture, you know? I've been spending some quality time with Matthew Robert from the fantastic industrial band New Rising Son. "They even sampled my voice on their new album." I take a kitten off my lap and ask Miss B how she sees her future. "My sole aspirations are to continue performing acting, music, and art. I'm living for it right now. If it turns out that I should marry and have ten children, then that is what will happen. If I die before the age of forty, that is how it will happen. I enjoy living. It's just the way I live; I know I can't carry on like this forever. When I go to goth clubs, people say, 'You can become one of us'. And I say, "If you think you can make me immortal with your vampire teeth, go for it, but I don't think it will happen." I wore an 'Outlaw' T-shirt the other day; I'm definitely a rebel. I really am the embodiment of someone who lives in the moment."

Chapter 14: The Male Groupie

I saw an old television episode where Dick Cavett interviewed Janis Joplin and inquired if she had any male groupies. She said, 'Not nearly enough', and I felt weirdly validated. So begins my first exciting conversation with Mr. Ian Wagner, also known as "Pleather". Our first meeting is held at the Farmers Market on Fairfax Avenue, a historic Hollywood landmark. For decades, I've frequented this legendary hotspot, sharing delicious turkey burgers and crab salad platters with Sparks' Ron and Russell Mael, my ex-husband Michael, and our son, Nick. Today, I proposed lunch at the Gumbo Pot. As I browse the delicious Cajun menu, I recommend that my guests order the wonderful oyster po'boy.

Pleather, who appears small and bashful, has brought along Drama, the disarming, outspoken platinum blonde bass player in the alldoll, straightedge (no drugs, no booze) band Switchblade Kittens. When I ask Pleather how he obtained such a distinctive nickname, he can't recall. Drama surely can: "It was the pants." He has these pleather pants that are really form fitting, and you can obviously see his endowments." Aha.

Pleather, 32, says that, despite his well-known stature, he has never been a showoff. "I'm not that kind, but what the hey, it's worked great for me. I had never considered myself a groupie until Drama informed me of the fact. I was simply living my life when I ran into a couple of her band members, or they ran into me. I began telling Drama all of my adventures, and she remarked, "You are a groupie." And I said, 'OK, I guess I am'. I never believed the term had a negative meaning, and now I am proud of it. People do not realise how much it is about the music. I'm not only turned on by a lady playing an instrument; it's the empathy I feel for the musician. I want to get close to the creative process. "That is all."

Pleather's admiration for his musical heroes appears to be identical to that of any female groupie I've interviewed. Can a guy become a muse? Why the Hell not?

"I grew up downstairs from Johnette Napolitano of Concrete Blonde. When I was eleven or twelve, her younger sister babysat me. She was also a musician—the usual '80s stoner, burnout girl. I was somewhat advanced for my age, and nature took its course. Following that event, I began pursuing it. I've only ever been attracted to ladies who are musicians. Ever. I've never been attracted to ordinary people. Never. I have tried it, but there is always something missing."

I tell Pleather that I've given it my all, but I always come back to the man on the pedestal, sorry, the stage—perhaps because my father was larger than life and seemed unapproachable.

"My relationship with my mother has completely formed and determined my life", Pleather recounts. "I was homeschooled, so we were always together and very close. She taught me how to play guitar and recommended books to read. She made me stay up late to see excellent films. She exposed me to every aspect of life and art. I had a peculiar grown-up quality about me. By the age of two, I was already reading. When I was six, I was continuously playing guitar. By the age of eight, I could socialise with my parents' friends and engage in academic conversations. My father always worked, provided, and did the "dad thing." He was a drummer for two or three bands. So practically every night, he went off to play. When I was ten, my parents established a punk band, and I attended all of their practices. This was 1981, and it was still very innovative. My mother plays guitar, bass, and keyboards, so I've always had an affinity for female musicians."

And which female band introduced Pleather to the secrets of love? "The Pandoras were the first all-girl band I had any meaningful experience with. They began as a garage band and eventually transitioned into metal. I was fifteen. They were in their late twenties and really eager to have a plaything in their midst. Things got extremely insane; they were really free and open—let's just say so. They were not shy and would indulge in couplings whenever and wherever it was appropriate. They'd do each other while you did them, bring another guy over, two for one, every combination imaginable. I went on tour with them and was basically their toy."

"On more than one occasion he coupled with the entire band", Drama reports.

"Yes, that happened," Pleather admits. "It's for the record".

"He's rock and roll's best-kept secret," Drama adds. "People don't realise he's the greatest feminist, and if you're going to have a band-aid, you might as well have Pleather on hand. Sure, you can have sex on the tour bus, but Pleather is the smartest man I've ever met. And he's wearing pink hot pants! But some female performers are terrified of him since he is known as "THE male groupie." I'm not sure if Pleather is happy or embarrassed by this little detail.

"When I was younger, I didn't understand female rockers were a novelty. I was of legal age when the Runaways, Joan Jett, Patti Smith, and Heart were released. Following the Pandoras, I moved on to Pleasant Gehman's band, the Screamin' Sirens. I believe Pleasant enjoyed treating men in the same way she had been victimised. I got the impression she was performing a role since she was so much wiser than the individuals she was following about. I've always thought she was better than Darby Crash and had a lot to say."

Pleather, I believe, had little trouble attracting the most desirable rock ladies because of his reputation.

"His reputation is that he has the biggest dick in rock and roll" , Drama hisses.

Pleather responds, "Don't believe the hype".

I'm sure many of Pleather's partners have been as impressed by his musical knowledge and understanding. "I've studied the history of music, and I believe whatever men had to say ended with punk rock, which is where women began. Women are saying everything that matters in rock music today. I've always wanted to be at the centre of the action. In 1990, no band generated more attention than L7. You'd walk into a bar where they were playing and feel as if the world was about to explode. They actually had something to say. They walked onstage, and it was absolute power. I have a lengthy history with them. I was their support system for several years, but it became a horrible experience since my emotions were manipulated. I went back and forth between three bandmates. And I loved them all at the same time, more than anything. I'd still be with any member of L7. An awful, unprotected mishap occurred, and one of them became pregnant. That was my indication to leave the scenario because they acted like a coven. They gossip about each other behind their backs, yet when anything comes into their lives, they simply close ranks. They would not respond to my phone calls. They'd simply stroll by me. It was heartbreaking since I considered them my family—sisters, lovers, and everything. So I said, 'That's it; I'm going to stay celibate from now on. "I am not getting emotionally involved."

He didn't lose heart, but Pleather soon found himself catering to another disturbed rock waif, Inger Lorre of the Nymphs, who is best known for being pissed off at her A&R man. Her album had been in the works for much too long, and she got up on the hapless fellow's desk and urinated all over it, setting a new standard for naughty rock behaviour. "I'd bring Inger to Perry Farrell's place to get heroin and assist her shoot up, which I knew went beyond the call of duty. She was extremely skilled, but she was suffering from bodily, spiritual, and mental torment. Heroin was the only thing keeping her away from it. We would watch Drugstore Cowboy five times in a row. I awoke one afternoon to find her breathing oddly slow, and I couldn't wake her up. I knew there was only a short time before she died, so I used the ice cube treatment on her bum. I ended up saving her life that day. That relationship lasted about six months, and it was clear that she could not be saved. She was one of those people who made you do everything she did, so I was using heroin alongside her. But I didn't take as much and managed to preserve my faculties."

Did Pleather believe it was his job to accommodate and encourage the ladies in his life?Of course. Jennifer Finch from L7 introduced me to Courtney Love, and I immediately recognized her as a poet. She'd open for L7, and I'd have to coach her before and after each show. She would say, 'I'm just not as good as L7. I'd tell her, 'You don't understand; you're going to be huge, the next Patti Smith or Madonna. You're going to be an icon! When I first met her, she was humble, and I believe she has maintained that throughout. I spent time with her when she was at odds with her guitarist, Eric. They had an on-and-off relationship, and he didn't mind what she did since he knew he couldn't stop her. He also worshipped her. But she put herself down. She handed it up to men. She does not believe she is as talented as she is, and she has been heavily influenced by Kurt, Billy Corgan, and Trent Reznor. All she needs to do is trust her artistic intuition. I ended up with Courtney, although it was more of a friendship/love relationship. I thought she was wonderful, and I slept with her, but it was all for pleasure. I hate to admit it, but she was rather normal in bed. She was not wild. I don't know, maybe I'm crazy, but she was nothing in comparison to the Pandoras—true Hollywood sleaze all around. But I have nothing negative to say about Courtney. I thought she was amazing.

"Later, two Pandoras formed the Muffs, a band that destroyed itself due to their egos. I was with Kim Shattuck for a spell. Kim was just like Courtney in that she would absolutely destroy everyone around her for her own ego. "No human emotions, just a robot."

Despite his commitments to himself to keep his emotions under control, Pleather fell down the rock and roll rabbit hole again in 1992. "I fell absolutely in love with Carla Bozulich, the lead vocalist of Geraldine Fibbers. I adore minds and creative spirits. She was everything I'd ever wanted and am still looking for—the undeniable love of my life. So Carla and I began off as friends, and it ended up being the longest romance I've ever had. I chased her, which was not something I was used to doing. She was a troubled genius, completely twisted up, which is exactly how I like them. "She needed a lot of help, and I enjoy assisting."

"He likes 'em cra-zee," Drama responds.

"I just wanted to help her from having to deal with the outside world. I wanted to remove anything that was getting in the way of her creativity. I adored the earth she walked on. I kept the circus running, and for a while it worked." Carla found someone else after just over two years of their ill-fated romance. "That was the worst," Pleather complains. "I've coped with family deaths before, but they weren't quite as painful as losing Carla. That was the one time I found myself standing on the overpass with one foot planted and one foot dangling. I went into a three-year hermetic period, with no sex or relationships. I worked as a bookshop clerk, read my books, and began writing. "I didn't even go out."

Pleather began writing I'm with the Girl Band as a kind of catharsis. "I was going to check with you to see if it would be okay," Pleather insisted. I guarantee him that I'll be first in line to purchase it.

Pleather began playing guitar in local bands when he was fifteen, and he continued to do so throughout his turbulent relationships. "Yeah, I always had my own bands and followed everyone else, but I never valued my music. For me, everything revolved around them. But after my hermetic phase, I said, 'OK, this is it, I'm focused too much on other people, I'm going to do my own thing'." But when he published an ad in the paper looking for "female friendly" musicians, he ended up being the only male in his new band. "I had that band, Roller Girl, for a few years and fell in love with Rosanna the drummer, which pretty much destroyed my life again" . Pleather sighed. "She was also in a goth band, so I became their aide and handled everything for them. Then she joined the Switchblade Kittens, and I met Drama. "That happened three years ago."

"He ended up splitting up with that drummer, then marrying our next drummer. In fact, he has dated, lived with, or married each of our drummers," Drama says. When I ask Drama how many drummers the Switchblade Kittens have gone through, her response cracks me up. "Seventeen! Pleather attempted to save seventeen insane drummer girls.

"You're kidding me, right?" . I'm puzzled: "This is beginning to sound like Spinal Tap!" . Pleather chuckles enthusiastically, "Yes! They spontaneously combust, and it's over! Seriously, caring for a drummer is a full-time job. Here's the main distinction I perceive between male and female groupies: all of the ladies I've met want to be talked to. They want someone to listen. I've always been empathetic. I enjoy listening and helping others. I don't believe most men place much stock in that. In many ways, I believe they simply want to use women."

"You can be a successful woman in rock and don't have to resort to getting back at men" , Drama asserts; "and some women have done that to Pleather" .

"That's exactly what happened," he confirms. "But I won't hold it against any of them. Anyway, when I go out now, I simply want to be myself. "I'm there to be seen and make an impression—to be fabulous."

Drama reaches into her purse and gives me a pastel pink Switchblade Kittens CD. She says the one they're now working on will be even better. "Pleather gives me confidence in the studio," she says, gently rubbing his palm.

"That's what I live for," he explains. "That is why I do what I do." It is natural for me. "I just need to be creative."

A few weeks later, on a dreary, rainy day, Pleather and I met for another heart-to-heart at a coffee shop in my old Reseda neighbourhood. I haven't been here in years, and it looks just like any other dull corner in the Valley. Pleather, on the other hand, stands out with his tight black outfit, beautiful leather cap, and splendid woolly scarf that highlights his high cheekbones. After hugging me, he says he's glad we're alone this time. "I didn't lie to you the last time, but there was drama. It was probably beneficial for you to see me like that since that's how I act when I'm with an artist I admire. I ended up letting her relate my story.

Pleather bravely brings me a vanilla latte, and we sit by the window, listening to the raindrops fall. "I was walking here, thinking about what to say. I've always had my own bands, but all I wanted to be was the guitarist in Blondie or Bjorn in Abba. I want to be the person who helps the goddess-female-artist-singer. When I read your book and reread it ten thousand times, I learned that there are both positive and negative aspects to the entire experience. My mother had such a tremendous influence on me from a young age that empathy is simply inbuilt in me. I've subconsciously shaped my entire life to play the conventionally feminine role in partnerships. When I say feminine, I mean the person who is perceived as weaker by the outside world but is actually the one driving things forward. Women make the world go 'round, but males get the credit. Pleather continues. "To me, the actual revolution of the 1970s was women taking on more powerful roles, not punk. Punk was simply a reassert of established beliefs. The true shift was the feminine phenomenon, but I was too young to recognize it. I'd turn on the TV and see Wonder Woman and Charlie's Angels, all these ladies with guns. I was like, 'Yeah! These rules!' I have every Wonder Woman season on DVD. I was watching an episode with Drama lately, and she interrupted Wonder Woman's motion. She tried to talk to me, but I said, 'I can't talk'. I had to turn around and face the other direction. Wonder Woman still has a deep impact on me. This is ridiculous! I had a fundamentally distorted image of women from a young age. Pop culture had a strong influence on me, and this was when the women's movement became more mainstream. It wasn't so much the manifesto or the bra-burning stuff. It's more like when it enters the pop mainstream, the revolution truly begins. I needed to be a part of it and be connected to the ultimate centre." Pleather laughs. "That's a rather sexual metaphor; I didn't intend it that way. There is only one thing that is ultimately greater. If you're not one of those people who thinks, 'I'm larger than life,' you should be with someone who is. The first moment I saw Courtney, I knew she was a genius. There was something about her that reminded me of Dylan or Patti Smith. People like that have an aura about them. "There is such a glow."

What, other than his God-given, spectacular physical endowment, drew the goddesses to Ian "Pleather" Wagner?

"I have a rescuing complex, and I choose the ones who are the most screwed up. A buddy of mine once said, "If Squeaky Fromme and Donna Reed were standing next to each other, you would go with Squeaky." And I replied, 'Yes, exactly'. I just want to assist, fix, and be the shoulder. I perceived Courtney as someone who was hurting, had true, honest female energy, was angry, and knowledgeable. She only needed to be informed how terrific she was. At the time, no one told her she was wonderful. No one. Every musician I knew would say, 'I can't believe you went to see Hole. They're the worst band I've ever seen. This was in the beginning, when they practised at my friend's house. L7 were supposed to be the next big thing, the great revolution band, with female rockers doing it. Courtney was stepping forward for them, and I needed to give her the confidence to continue. Every time she performed, I would be there. It became ludicrous. One club was so broken down that they only had one microphone stand. The stand broke halfway through the show, and Courtney replied, 'Well, I guess the show's done. I said, 'No, let me hold it' and picked it up. I was trying to rock out while also holding the microphone stand for her. "How metaphorical can you get?" He chuckles: "No, that's beyond metaphor; it's too literal" .

So what is the secret? How did he go from holding her microphone stand to getting inside her panties?

"There's a lot of truth in certain caricatures about how women and men interact with one another. Women essentially want to be heard and empathised with. They want to be hard, tough, and in control at times, but not all the time. I've always had a sixth sense for knowing when to be the listener — essentially, the girlfriend — and when to return to the manly role. I believe this has contributed to my success with women. They're not used to having a guy deflate his own ego. Women rarely have the opportunity to experience this. It has to do with locating a sympathetic soul. It's like spirits in transit. You might be on a different road, but that's fine as long as you have that one experience, that one night. The finest time I had with Courtney was simply kissing. We were sitting in front of a club, cars were passing by, everyone inside was getting drunk, and I had 10 minutes alone with her, kissing and making out." Pleather's sleepy expression indicates that he is enjoying this particular sensory recollection.

"That feeling is something I've been chasing ever since. "That was probably the most romantic and sweetest experience I've ever had." Pleather pauses and smiles, "I guess that's kind of sad".

I understand perfectly. He shared a poignant moment with his icon, which has become one of those really uncommon snapshot memories.

"Actually, I have had very few sexual situations that did not involve a lot of emotional exchange. Women's emotions are very close to the surface, and when you tap into them, everything comes flooding out. Female musicians have a lot of trouble communicating. And if you're interested, they'll gladly share their emotions, hearts, and bodies with you."

Even if Pleather's heart has been destroyed a few times, it appears like the pain and suffering was worthwhile. "Oh, that is the major thing I want to say. No matter how horribly I was treated—and I was treated badly by many of them—there isn't a single lady I have anything against. We are all just trying to do our best and make our lives work. It was an honour to be among them even for a short period of time. It was my joy. "I'd give any of them my last two dollars."

Pleather surprised me before we open our umbrellas and brave the Reseda rain. "I've joined the Switchblade Kittens," he says proudly. "I'm co-writing and co-producing their album, and it's coming out terrific. I can't tell you how fulfilling that is. I am also co-directing their documentary. There is a lot going on with that band. "They're like a multimedia, crazy circus."

I had to inquire. Is he dating the drummer?

"No, no, no," he assures me with a laugh. "For once in my life, I am going to strive to keep business and pleasure separate. And I've discovered that the grass isn't always greener over there. We tend to favour other people's stories over our own. We value the insane, visionary genius, and artistic individuals. We're attracted by them and wonder, 'Oh my God, where does she get such ideas?' Of course, I'm still fascinated by it and will always be. And I make no apologies for pursuing my ambition. But hopefully, the natural balance begins to emerge, and you learn to value your own experience and see your own worth." Pleather pauses for a time, gazing into the black winter sky, before smiling at me, "But I still adore Lynda Carter. If I saw her, I would simply... "I would..." I would simply collapse and die. "All I've been looking for is Wonder Woman with a guitar!"

Chapter 15: Miss You in a Heartbeat

In the thick of winter, with snow squalls swirling around my head, I'm glad to leave the beautiful coastlines of California and take a plane to the cold Midwest. I've been exchanging emails with a few active groupies in Minneapolis and have decided to meet up. It's a long journey, but I genuinely enjoy exploring all of America and meeting new dolls that share my interests. When I arrive at the Minneapolis-St. Paul airport, I burrow into my enormous faux-fur coat, hire a small Toyota, check into a Holiday Inn Express, and contact Sarah Madison, a savvy-sounding hottie in her early twenties. She proposes that we meet at a neighbouring seafood restaurant in the same massive mall where she works at the local Hooters.

Sarah has sent me images of herself, casually posing next to wild-eyed rocker boys from Tantric, Sevendust, and Marilyn Manson's band, so I recognize her immediately. She is tall and willowy, with long, straight platinum hair and a knowing greeneyed expression. After an embrace, we settle into a booth, order a couple of exotic tropical drinks, and I immediately discover that she isn't a fan of the G word. "I dislike that word. But sometimes I think 'Band Aid' is fine. However, any label indicates that I am only friends with or drawn to these people because they are renowned. Working for a music magazine exposes you to very few individuals outside of the rock and roll community. Until I moved here, I was in Madison, Wisconsin, writing feature articles and reviewing CDs for Maximum Ink music magazine—'All Access with Sarah'. Who knew that kids really want to know what kind of beer Nickelback drinks? Yes, Corona". Sarah chuckles.

Even though she claims to understand the on-the-road rocker mindset, Sarah's heart was just broken by one of those seductive, irresponsible boys. "This happened in December. I had already considered talking to you, but I did not want to identify names. Following that incident, I changed my mind. I realised these folks don't care about me. So, why do I care about defending their reputations?"

How did the stunning daughter of a "big-shot lawyer" who graduated at the top of her class end herself backstage? "On my sixteenth birthday, I received Vault: Greatest Hits 1980-1995 and Adrenalize by Def Leppard, and bang! I never turned back. My first real concert was Def Leppard. I told my partner after the event, 'Oh my God, during this one section in this one song, Joe Elliott definitely stared directly at me!' That's funny to think that was such a huge deal back then."

Although Sarah did not meet her heroes that night, she was captivated by genuine live rock and roll. "When I first started attending concerts, I couldn't help but notice the chick on the side of the stage. She looks amazing, she's drinking her beer, and she's simply thrilled to be there. I thought it would be awesome to be that girl. My roommate and I went to see Almost Famous, and there's this moment in the Hyatt House where Penny Lane walks around and everyone recognizes her. I thought, 'God, that's awesome'. It feels nice to be the person that people want to talk to, whether in the rock world or anywhere else. We met the band Oleander while they performed in Madison. They were in Milwaukee the next night and invited us. We stayed in the back drinking with them until they got on. They were on stage before we even left the dressing room. We walked out, and three girls looked at us like, 'You lucky bitches,' and I thought, 'Wow, I made it. "I'm the chick I used to be jealous of."

Sarah's attractive, wholesome appearance frequently drew the attention of roadies looking for appetising treats. "We were still in high school." I never approached roadies and asked, 'Hey, can I flash you for a pass?'. But, recall, I was at a heavy metal show. First and foremost, it is made up of 75% men. Second, 90% of the girls weigh 300 pounds and wear Korn T-shirts from 1995. We were naturally noticeable. I've always wanted to be up front. There's a rush to make eye contact. You listen to this music all day in your bedroom, and the individuals who created it are staring right at you. It's not them as individuals, but what they've produced. After that, I tried to be the coolest rocker chick. The first time I gained confidence, I was in the front row of a Slipknot concert because I had to be there. A roadie approached and said, 'You, come back here'. So I observed from the side of the stage. If I wanted to meet or spend time with someone, I wouldn't approach them and start gushing about how wonderful they were. I would say, "I really enjoyed the show." Can I buy you a drink? If they were chatting to someone, I'd say, 'I'll be over there. Come over when you want that drink. "They enjoy that."

Sarah had an adoring high school lover, but she was hesitant to get too close to him. "I suppose that's what I enjoyed about musicians—you can be really close for a day. It's perfect. For one day, you are a boyfriend and girlfriend who are completely in love. Then they leave. You have all the nice things and none of the bad. It's all fun and games until you attempt to be serious. "That is when you get hurt."

I point out that the majority of the groupies I know have different opinions. A night or two with their idols is simply not enough. "I've always been really practical about it. Early on, a few people duped me. I thought, 'Oh, he really likes me!' But deep down, I knew exactly what was going on. Still, sometimes I'd lie in bed wondering, 'Wouldn't it be awesome if this happened?' However, the majority of these men live with spouses or girlfriends. Why would I want to be involved with a person who is cheating on his girlfriend?

Didn't she feel guilty? "It's not like they'll fall in love and then want to leave their marriages. I'm not going to disrupt their relationships."

No matter how much I beg, Sarah refuses to reveal the name of her first rock amour. "I'll tell you about the second one I met: Marilyn Manson's guitar player, John 5. It was a tour bus experience, and a memorable one. It wasn't like we had something big going on, but he's a great guy. I still have a lot of love for him. But I was actually at the show to watch Buckcherry that evening. I made my way to the front, and someone on the other side of the barricade had a video camera. I smiled at him, and he said, 'I don't want you to flash or anything; just say hello to the camera. An hour later, he saw me and said, "I showed Manson and John your tape." They truly want to meet you. I thought, "How brilliant!" They sent someone out with a video camera. That's so rock & roll. I was fresh to the music scene and a little terrified of Manson, but I went to the meeting spot with thirty other girls. They led us to this room, and all these girls were asking, "Do you have any beer?" God, why is there no beer? I'm not high-maintenance, and I believe John loved that about me. Finally, they pointed to me and three girls in bikinis. We got to the bus, and I had no idea what to do. I was nineteen years old! Manson was sitting there with Twiggy and John, and I was in amazement. But I took a long breath and thought, "These people are no better than me." We are all human. I approached and said, 'What's up? I'm Sarah, and he said, 'I'm Manson. I said hello to Twiggy, sat down, and began talking to John. I wasn't flirting; we were just laughing at the bikini girls because Manson was saying, 'Why don't you do this to him and that to him? And they said, 'OK!' After that performance, the girls were booted off the bus, and I thought, 'Wow, it really is like VH1!' John and I were simply attracted to each other. We had a wonderful experience. A few weeks later, I saw him at Ozzfest. Meanwhile, I'd started dating Glen Sobel, another tour participant. "He played drums for Beautiful Creatures."

Aha. Rockstar number three appears. "I saw him in the same way that you would see someone on tour with Ozzfest. We talked on the phone. Glen was a nice man, and we were actually seeing each other—but the tour ended, and owing to location, we didn't see each other for years. But we are still good friends. Then it was the start of the end". Sarah sighs deeply. "Lajon Witherspoon from Sevendust was the first person to absolutely mislead me. Until then, I'd had some wonderful encounters. But I know Lajon now, and he's definitely the most important player in the game. The females allowed him to act that way. The first time we met at a concert, I recognized him because he is the only black man in hard rock. He was signing signatures, so I gave him my ticket stub to sign. He said, "You have to hang out with me tonight." Do you own a pass? Come with me right now," and he whisked me backstage. God, he plays the game so brilliantly. We went on the bus, and he introduced me to his band. A security guy escorted me to the edge of the stage and placed me very next to the speaker. When you're not used to this, you think, 'Oh my God, I'm enjoying life!' The band's singer said, 'I want her right here—close to me'. He was getting set to go on stage when the tour manager shouted, 'You can't wear those jeans without a belt; hop up and down three times. He did, and half of his buttocks were exposed. I was wearing a dazzling, sparkly belt, so I handed it to him and he wore it on stage. I thought, 'That's my belt!' He said, 'I'm delighted I got this because now you have to see me thereafter. "He kept coming over to me during the show, and my heart was racing."

Sarah became tipsy, but just made out with Lajon that night, and he vowed to invite her to the next local performance. "The day approaches, and I don't seem to have received a phone call. But I went to find out what was going on. We were hanging out after the show when my best friend said, 'Turn around'. I answered, 'No, I'm not going', and she said, 'Just turn around'. So I turned around, and there was Lajon, turning on the charm again: 'Come here, I'm so sorry'. His justification was that 9/11 had occurred and everyone's mind was in a different place. That was the first time we hooked up. It was a fast tour bus romance, and he was going to call me again, right? Nothing. We drive to Chicago to see them, and I'm so mad, thinking, 'God, I hate him, I hate him', but of course I'm at the show."

Lajon apologised again, saying Sarah had attempted to contact her at Hooters. "We're not supposed to get personal calls, so the female hung up on him, and I never received the message. Lajon and I only spent the night together once because they had a hotel. It was just beautiful. That night, he was remarkable.

In my groupie days, hardly many bands used tour buses, and I remarked that intimacy on the road must be much more difficult nowadays. "Yeah, but most musicians are accustomed to receiving it all the time. I should give Lajon a break because the bus was often crowded, so we were in the bathroom. There isn't much love to be had in the frickin' tour bus restroom. However, that night in the hotel was excellent. It was December, and he asked what I wanted for Christmas. At the very least, I had one night that made me quite pleased. Of course, the next night they played Milwaukee, and did he even call me to add me to the roster after our amazing night? No. We got on the list through someone else. I approached Morgan Rose, the drummer, and asked, 'Where the fuck's Lajon?' He responded, 'Oh, he went to bed already'. I said, "Sure he did." The next time I saw him, I said, "Fuck you, Lajon." How dare you send your drummer to do the dirty work! When I walked into the women's bathroom at the House of Blues, he was sitting with four chicks. He said, 'Hello, everyone. This is Sarah. The one I've been talking about. I say, 'Yeah, right'. I wish I could say I didn't see him again after that. But I saw him many more times. He even came to my apartment."

Sarah was discovering that you can't rely on rock guys in the long run, but she decided she could still have fun. "I believe people are more interested in confidence than anything else, and if you happen to have good face features to back it up, that is fine. But having a dude on the cover of Rolling Stone wanting to hang out with you doesn't knock your confidence one bit. My friend and I will be standing among a group of twenty girls, and they will notice. 'What about these two? They'll be OK. They like it if you've done it previously because you understand what's proper and what isn't. For example, don't poop on the bus and don't flush your toilet paper. That is a terrible thought. Hmm. Where do you keep your toilet paper on the tour bus? So, who came along to take Sarah's mind off of Lajon?

"There were many flings that lasted a couple of weeks. Jeff Labar is Cinderella's guitarist. We got along right away and had a great time. We always made each other laugh. We were wonderfully compatible—just as you will be on the Poison summer tour. Then there was Jason 'Gong' Jones, the lead singer of Drowning Pool—he was hip. He chased me briefly, but I replied, 'Honey, you're releasing an album in a few months. You're about to go big. I'm not going to pretend we could have a relationship."

Sarah was meticulous in following her keep-it-fun rule until one of the rockers treated her too well. "I had been seeing this guy from Dope, Sloane 'Mosey' Jentry, casually. When he left the band, I kept acquainted with the rest of the guys, and they hired Brix as his replacement. You're supposed to stay with one guy per band, but I made an exception since Brix was incredible. He treated me quite well. He took me out to dinner, then we went to the performance, and he handed me about $30 and said, 'Here, this should buy you drinks till I'm ready to hang out'. We were seeing each other frequently, and I began to feel guilty because he was married. As far as his wife knew, he was simply 'wham, bam, thank you, ma'am' on the road. But if she had known he was taking me out to supper...

Dope was playing Madison, and as far as Sarah knew, everything was OK between her and Brix. "I'm waiting after the show. When he finally appeared, I said, 'What the fuck is going on?' He said, 'Let's go speak about it. I've been thinking, and I don't think we're compatible anymore. I said, 'That's obviously a lie. If he'd said, "I think you have an ugly vagina and I never want to see it again," I'd have been far less outraged than if he tried to deceive me. Was he watching Sex and the City last night for horrible breakup lines? We surely did not appear to be incompatible two weeks ago when we were getting it on. So that was the end of it. A week later, I texted him, 'When you're ready to share the truth, I'm ready to listen'. He left me a voicemail saying, 'I'm delighted you phoned. I genuinely want to chat to you. Then I spotted their drum tech at Hooters, and he said, "Hey, Brix wants your number." He wants to apologise, but I haven't heard anything from him. But he made me realise that they were all the same. Even if they appear to be nice individuals, they are all the same. "That's when I decided to conduct this interview."

Sarah seems to have had enough of rock stars, particularly married ones. "For the time being," she agrees. "It was a part of my life that I thoroughly enjoyed. But I'm bored of it. I need something real, and you won't find it there. But I know that the moment I say, 'Oh no, I'll never date another musician,' some guy on a national tour will sweep me off my feet. I genuinely believe I have spent my life without regrets. If I ever think, 'Should I, or shouldn't I? I usually do. How many times have you looked back and said, 'God, if only I had done that'?

Yes, I recall the precise moment Jimi Hendrix beckoned to me, but I declined. Of course, I was a very inexperienced seventeen-year-old virgin at the time. Noel Redding, the charming, skinny, pale-faced bassist, seemed like a safer pick.

"I still dream, because I have more in common with musicians than with accountants" , Sarah replies. "It's more about the style than anything else. I enjoy the piercings and tattoos. I enjoy the unique hairstyle. Everyone has their top five guys they'd like to sleep with. It isn't a pipe dream for me. I think, 'This may possibly happen'. Joe Perry is my number one. Then Lenny Kravitz was my number two till I learned he doesn't smell so wonderful. But I'm thinking, 'I'll cover my nose; just bring me that dude and his PA!'"

Does Sarah ever see herself twenty years from now, all comfy with her crazy, tattooed rocker boyfriend? "You have to look at the facial features," she adds with a knowing smile. "Because he may look pretty hot now with all that hair, but you have to imagine that schnoz on your kid!".

After dinner, we head over to Sarah's pristine, spacious condo to peruse her extensive rock scrapbooks. She opens a cold bottle of white wine and pours us a glass. "This is me and Jeff from Cinderella, thirty seconds after we met..." Here's Jason from Drowning Pool. Here are the feathers from Ozzfest that Ozzy blew up at the conclusion... This is Glen from Beautiful Creatures. Ahh, look at Tommy Lee! I've never been so star-struck in my life. He was trying to talk to us, but we kept stuttering. He finally said, 'All right, great meeting you guys' and began to walk away. My friend was like, 'P-p-picture!' If Tommy Lee wanted to have some children, I would be delighted to oblige. Oh, these are the guys from Nickelback. I did not hook up with any of them. But I kissed Nick. Oh, this is a beautiful shot, since when I first arrived to Madison, we went to see Tantric and took a picture with the singer, Hugo Ferreira. We walked back, exclaiming, 'Oh, he's so dreamy'. Two years later, I hooked up with him. The night before, I had been hanging out with their drummer, Matt Taul. We were hanging together, and he got me into the show. I was looking for him and asked Hugo, 'Where's Matt?' He answered, 'Just get on the bus'. I refused because it makes you look like an idiot. So he said, 'Come with me'. It was Matt, Hugo, and I, and we were watching porn. I said sarcastically, "Dude." "This is really fun." I had a romance with Hugo on the bus that night, and the next day we traveled to Chicago. We had a great day because we were able to get a motel room that night. Hugo is amazing, and he smells great in the morning. "He's that guy right there," she continues, pointing to another image of the arrogant bad boy. "If I was going to be unrealistic and wanted one of them to change and be the guy, it'd definitely be him".

I've noticed that all of the younger groupies refer to sleeping together as "hooking up". "Right," Sarah replies. "To me, the term 'hooking up' carries less weight and strain. It progresses in sequence as it becomes more relationship-focused. You start with 'hooking up', then sleeping together', 'having sex', and finally making love'."

Where do blow jobs come in, I'm curious. "I am not sure. I suppose that might be considered hooking up. But I rarely do this. I am like,

'Uh-uh, buddy!'" I am amazed. Not even when she is crazy over someone? "No, at that point, I've already got 'em," Sarah says, "so why do I need to impress them anymore?" "I see no pleasure in that."

I ask Sarah if she browses groupie message boards on the Internet. "I'm not going to say anything, but you can bet your ass I read the discussion boards, particularly Metal Sludge. I am sure you have heard of this chick named Rikki Sixx. Let's just say she probably wet herself out of enthusiasm when she won 'Sludgette of the Month'. She's said she's in love with Taime Downe and has hung out with him roughly thirty times. Then she abruptly posted on the bulletin board, 'I BLEW TIME'. I was thinking, 'Taime does not want anyone to know that'. Have you seen the sex tape between Kid Rock and Scott Stapp? It's as if you couldn't detest Scott Stapp anymore. They show him sitting back and saying things like, 'It's fantastic to be the king…this is my third one today'. Where was that girl's self-esteem? I mean, go ahead and sleep with him. But she allowed herself to be filmed sucking him off while he said such derogatory things. Like I said, I don't do that very often."

I inform Sarah that Miss Tina, the second child I'm visiting today in Minneapolis, is proud of her oral abilities and enjoys climbing onboard the bus to express her gratitude. "But when she leaves, they'll probably talk a lot of crap about her," Sarah says, drinking her wine. "When I leave, at best, they'll say nice things, and at worst, they'll say nothing" .

Chapter 16: In So Deep

Miss Tina King is persistent. She has called multiple times to ensure I have the correct directions to her home on the other side of town. When I arrive and park in the crunchy snow, Tina greets me on the porch, smiling cheerfully. She's a little over five feet tall, with short pixie blonde hair and impish dimples, and she appears to be about to burst with happiness.

Tina has swamped me with emails about her exploits, and of all the girls I've met, she is the most upbeat and eager about the prospect of sharing her stories. "Oh, I just can't believe you're here!" she says as she hugs me fiercely and leads me into the modest wooden house she shares with her mother, Debbie, and her four-year-old daughter, Amber. Debbie greets me with a large grin. Little Amber has Autism Spectrum Disorder, and while she enjoys playing with her toys, she rarely interacts with me.

Tina and I talked about my desire to rummage through antique shops and thrift stores in search of buried treasure before arriving in Minneapolis. So the first thing we intend to do on this miserably chilly afternoon is browse around Goodwill and Salvation Army stores together. While Tina prepares to go, I see an eight-by-ten photo of her with Kid Rock hanging above the large television set. Debbie motions me to her and whispers in my ear. "Tina gave Kid Rock a B-L-O-W-J-O-B," she proudly adds, spelling out the letters before gazing over at Amber. "She can't spell, but you can't be too careful" . For the first time in years, I am speechless. Debbie doesn't appear to notice and pulls up Tina's high school newspaper, The Bluffer, from November 4, 1988. She refers to a short piece titled "Time Will Tell—Imagine a world-famous professor who invented a machine that can answer any question about the future." Tina King: "Will I ever reign as a groupie queen and appear on the cover of Rolling Stone?" Tina's English class assignment characterises Richie Sambora's guitar playing as "Magician's fingers produce auras of tone to mesmerise the fans." I'm struck by Debbie's comfort with her daughter's, shall we say, accomplishments, and I'm full of admiration for this open-minded mother.

While we are browsing antique stores, I ask Tina how her mother came to be so accepting. "She divorced when I was fourteen and has never remarried. We'd go to concerts and meet rock stars together. I would take her backstage. We shared a preference for the same genres and musicians. At first, I'd say, "Hello, guys, this is Debbie." But if I hung out with a band more than once, I'd eventually say, 'Guys, this is my mom'. They would say, 'Oh, that's pretty wonderful. But, since Amber's birth, Mom has usually stayed at home with daughter.

Tina's upbeat demeanour betrays her rough beginning and laser-focused dedication. She already holds a master of arts in human development and is on her way to earning a master's degree in social work. The position she intends to obtain is pretty unique. "I'd like to work at a veterinary facility where I could lead a grief and support group for people who have lost a pet or recently learned that their pet has a terminal illness. That combines my two great loves, animals and people, in one location."

Pretty impressive for a girl who claims to come from a "dirt poor" household. "My parents divorced when I was four. My mother married a travelling salesman when I was seven and was often gone, so my grandmother raised me. I was fairly good at keeping things hidden from my grandmother. I would sneak away and party. Where I grew up, if you weren't wealthy, no one noticed you, therefore I didn't have any boyfriends. I was quite smart, but I was a stoner. I hung together with potheads but maintained high grades. Later on, my mother was a single parent receiving welfare and food stamps. She worked at a bar for $2 an hour and didn't make enough money to support us, so we moved in with my grandparents and uncle. The five of us shared a one-bedroom house. My mother and I grew up as friends. We adored Dokken and all of the '80s hair bands. They were excellent showmen. I thought glam rock males with makeup, spandex, and big hair were quite attractive. I started following them around and realised they were at sound check between two and four o'clock. So I would go hang out near the buses. I would dress seductively and flamboyantly, and it always drew their attention. I'd shout, 'Hey!' and they'd send out their tour manager to find me. Many times, security would try to prevent me from getting to the bus by telling me to stay behind the yellow line. The police tape reads 'Do not cross'. But the rock artists would constantly say, 'She's with us.' "

We're browsing the local Goodwill when Tina points out a pair of black patent leather Mary Janes. "These will look so cute on Amber," she exclaimed excitedly. After checking out with our goodies, we stop for a cup of coffee and some rock nostalgia. Her first huge crush was Jon Bon Jovi, but she couldn't approach him. "It was like getting through a vault trying to meet the guy" , Tina relates. "My first sexual contact with a rock celebrity was with Tesla's guitarist, Tommy Skeoch. It was horrific, very methodical, with no foreplay—he simply pulled my clothes down. We were in the very rear of his tour bus, and he did not use a condom or kiss me. It lasted 10 minutes. "It was horrible."

Tina was understandably disappointed, and her crush on Tommy ended abruptly.

"Every month, the editor of Metal Edge magazine asked a group of rock stars the same question. This specific question was, 'What genuinely scares you about being a rock star?' Tommy responded, 'All the various ladies I've slept with without protection. When I read that, a shiver ran down my spine. So I wrote him a long letter and addressed it to the record label. I saw him about two months later. I received a backstage pass and was mingling with fans and talking to the other members of the band. Tommy stepped over to me and said, 'I got your letter'. He looked at me as if he could see into the depths of my soul. But I didn't say anything, I just left."

I ask Tina why she continued to go backstage after such a bad first encounter. "It is an addiction. Some people skydive, but I'm scared my parachute won't open. Meeting a rock star and indulging in an intimate, sexual deed is a thrilling experience because it makes me feel unique. I feel like I'm one of the chosen ones. When I was a newborn, my mother held me on the front porch while listening to 1970s music. So I grew up admiring the folks that make that music. It touches my heart. It speaks to my soul, and I desire a piece of that individual. I want to take a piece from them and incorporate it into me. A sexual act is the epitome of interweaving. After it happens, I see them on television or in publications and think, "I had a piece of that." I was with that individual. My desire has always been to marry a rock star. I never worried about what my career will be. I simply wanted to be a rock star wife or girlfriend. That has been my goal since I was a child."

But how would she feel about her rock honey hooking up with people like her while on the road? "I understand, that comes with the territory. But they would spend the most of their time with me. I don't care about money or being in the spotlight. Just having them as my private rock star, singing to me at 3am Rock stars are a unique species of free-spirited gipsies who march to the beat of their own inner drums. There aren't many musicians in my little town, so I went elsewhere to hang with the bands. It was the nicest vacation I'd ever had, and it provided an escape from my own bleak existence. I heard it in the halls and had it taped to my locker: 'You're a slut groupie'. I had to deal with that throughout high school, and it sucked. So, when I eventually met the band, got the laminate, and saw the same bitches who labelled me a slut, I could tell them, 'Now look who's the slut, bitches?' They wanted to meet the bands and would try to brown nose me, 'Oh, Tina!' How have you been? I do not think so. Ha ha ha. Payback is a motherfucker, isn't it? Revenge is a sweet medicine. I understand that wasn't polite, but they weren't good to me either."

Tina's eleven-year-old husband was hardly a rock star, but he was definitely a different breed. "He was a Norwegian pilot, and unlike the other guys in my small town, he had virtually white hair, was tall and slim, and had a dimple on his chin. I was almost twenty-one when I married him because he was unique. But being a groupie was one thing I would not give up, and he despised it. He would stress out for a week every time a band came to our region. My second sexual rock celebrity encounter was with Bill Leverty, the bass player for Firehouse. I gave him a blow job but did not finish. He exclaimed, 'Oh, jeez, don't do this to me'. He was prepared to get blue balls. I answered, 'I can't. I am married. I have to go. Good-bye!' As I was running off the bus, he cried, 'You've already cheated, so finish!' I felt terrible. It is sad to say, yet it was still enjoyable. He's hot! I told my hubby because I am an open person. I cheated on him again with the guitar player for Survivor. I returned to his hotel room after the show, where we swam and had sex. I did not inform my husband about that one until a week later."

Tina went to performances and partied with band members, but she remained faithful until her marriage fell apart. "After my divorce, '80s bands were making a comeback, playing small clubs. So the next one was five years ago, and it was Phil Lewis, the singer for the Los Angeles Guns. A lot of groupies nickname him 'Philthy' Lewis, so he travels. But I believe I genuinely fell in love with him. The first time I gave him a blow job on the bus. The following time we had sex. He's a great lover, and it wasn't just nasty sex. He cared for me. The concert was spectacular. I was in the front row centre, and at the end of the play, he looked at me and said, 'Thanks, Tina,' before bending down on one knee and kissing me in front of everyone. I thought, 'Oh my God, it doesn't get any better! "This will never happen again." We did things that were not like the other rock stars' sex acts. For example, he met my mother. A few months later, he came over to my house to take a shower. I just knew he lived in a posh neighbourhood in Los Angeles and owned a home and expensive sports vehicles. I was ashamed since some of the tile in my bathroom had fallen off, but I couldn't say no because he needed to shower. He'd seen my mother before, so they were chatting, and I contacted my friend Angie, who was driving me to the show in her yellow Volkswagen. I said, "Somebody else is here, and he also needs a ride." She asked, 'Who is he?' I replied, 'Phil Lewis'. She arrived and was all starry-eyed. We drove to the show with the sunroof open. It was odd since we had grown up listening to him, and I never imagined I'd be having sex with him seventeen years later. Not once or twice, but four times. After the play, we boarded the tour bus and had sex in one of the small bunk beds. It reminded me of the Japanese hotel cubicles I'd seen in movies, but it was surprisingly comfortable. It was cramped quarters, but it worked. There was a curtain, so we had privacy. And we weren't being too loud. We were respectful since we were aware of everyone else on the bus. I once spent a weekend with him. I took off work to go to the Super 8. There were three tour buses in the parking lot, and I wasn't sure which one was theirs. So I stayed in my tiny red Ford Aspire, thinking, 'I'll just wait until some rock celebrity gets off the bus. Tracii Guns, L.A. Guns' former guitarist, was present. He's currently in Brides of Destruction. He'd seen me several times while hanging out with Phil. I said, "Tracii, could you please tell Phil to call Tina?" This is my room number 301'. I checked into the same hotel and floor. So Phil came to my room, and we took a candlelit bath, which was very lovely. We sat there and discussed our personal lives. He told me that he wrote the song 'Crazy' about his ex-wife, who had mental issues. It's a fantastic song since one of the lines says, 'Don't call me crazy. We played about in the bathtub, but it didn't go so well because guys struggle to achieve orgasms in bathtubs. At least that's what I've discovered from my experience. So he placed the candles alongside the bed on the nightstand. I gave him a blow job, and as we were having sex, the tip of the pillowcase touched the candle flame, catching fire. I couldn't think or move, but he was quite quick to react. He beat the pillow on the carpet, and the fire was finally extinguished, but there was a massive hole with no carpet. I replied, 'Oh, shit. I'm going to have to pay for property damage. But Phil put the table over the burned area, so I was completely out of that one. A few hours later, he invited me to his room, where Brent Muscat of Faster Pussycat was present. They were hungry, so we visited Perkins. And that was extremely fantastic since I was out to breakfast with two well-known rock stars. Everyone was staring, and a lot of people continued approaching the table. I was so nervous that I couldn't eat. It's strange: I could have the sex because it's second nature, but here I was, sitting with two rock artists I admired as a kid, and I had no idea what to say. Basically, I listened to them talk and sipped my pop. We returned to the hotel room, and Phil proposed a threesome. I felt a little uneasy because I genuinely liked him. I questioned if I should do it because what if he lost respect for me? At the same time, I was excited and thrilled by the concept. So I simply went for it, and it was OK. Brent was shy, which shocked me. He acted like a schoolboy, not knowing what he was doing. Phil acted more aggressively. I gave Brent a blowjob, and Phil and I kissed for a bit. Brent and I started having sex, but I stopped, so we didn't finish. Then Phil and I had sex, while Brent walked away and did his own thing. They'd been excellent friends for years, and it didn't appear to be an issue for them. I don't think it was their first threesome. I wondered if they were bisexual. I saw a video camera and was concerned that he had put it to record. I still have a strong suspicion that there is a video of us. I would like to get my hands on it and destroy it—or preserve it! The following day, I told Phil As I was leaving, he said he wanted to chat to me. He said,

'I think you're a really wonderful girl, and I don't want your heart destroyed. "I can't give you what you need."

Tina continued to hang out with the band whenever they came through town, and one night, it appeared Phil had changed his mind. "He asked, 'Do you want to meet up after the show?' But that never happened because at the end of the night, I gave a blow job to Metal Church's singer, Ronnie Munro. Stephen Pearcy's drummer then flirted with her, saying, 'You're stunning. Do you want to hang out? So we ended up getting into my minivan, and I also gave him a blow job."

But why was she with two different males when she could have been with her favourite? Tina shrugs, "I don't know". "I wanted something unusual and interesting. I suppose I wanted to add more notches to my belt. Hey, I might as well get them all. I thought it was cool that I received one from each band. Except for the one I desired most."

But wasn't she concerned that Phil would find out? "No, since I did not give those men my name. I don't believe the opening bands would inform the headliners because they compete for the same ladies' attention. It's competitive in that sense, like a turf battle."

The next night, Tina brings me to one of her favourite strip mall rock clubs, where we dance to a '70s cover band, swaying our booties like disco idiots. She tells me about Amber's father, a local dark-haired singer with whom she had a brief romantic relationship. Fortunately, they stay cordial, and he sees Amber frequently. Afterward, we drive around until we find an open IHOP so we can complete our conversation. Tina, a devout vegetarian, orders grilled cheese in the middle of the night, while I indulge in an awful, gooey dish of whipped cream-slathered pancakes.

Because she gives head so frequently, I suppose Tina genuinely enjoys performing oral sex. "It's a powerful thing," she confesses openly, "especially if the male enjoys it. If he climaxes quickly, I get this surge. Musicians have had plenty of it, and if you can thrill them, you think, 'Wow, I'm quite good at this. "I rock!" I enjoy discovering who is easy and who is not. If it's more difficult, that's a challenge."

I'm curious whether she's ever been unable to complete her conquest. "No. I employ the deep throat approach because I do not have a gag reflex. I swallow if they ask. Otherwise, I avoid it since it is bitter, salty, and unpleasant. Usually, I wait until the last second before moving my face. Or I let them land on my breasts. That is a huge rush for some guys. Of course, with Kid Rock, it was all over my face.

We've finally gotten to the infamous Kid Rock story. "In the second week of August 2000, I took a buddy to his show to celebrate her thirtieth birthday. We were in the fifth row, and his tour manager was constantly gazing at me, so I flirted back. He approached us and said, "You ladies, sit up here." Kid Rock only wants to stare at the stunning women in the front row. We could almost touch him, and he glanced directly at me, so I flashed him. He appeared to like it, as we soon received all-access passes. We walked backstage after the event, and there was an amazing buffet. When Kid Rock arrived, we snapped selfies with him, and I whispered, 'Do you wanna have a threesome?' He replied, 'No, thank you, but it's very nice of you to ask. There were so many stunning strippers flirting with him. I knew he could have his pick of the litter, but I kept making eye contact. Then I used my beer bottle to simulate fellatio. It went fully down, until the bottle was no longer visible. I could tell by the way he looked at me that he was turning on."

Kid Rock was quite fascinated and had his roadie invite Tina to pay him a visit in the back of the bus. "I was very nervous because I assumed I was going to meet a roadie or the guitarist. I walked in, and Kid Rock was alone. He said, 'You can close the door'. He was standing there with only a white towel wrapped around his waist, moisture on his chest and stomach, and wet hair, and he was very sexy. I asked, "Are we going to have sex?" He replied, 'No, I saw you with that beer bottle and want to check if you're as good as you appear to be. So I gave him a blow, and he responded, 'Can I come on your face?' I assured him, "Yes, you can do whatever you want." He grabbed a towel and cleaned my face, wiping it. 'Are you OK?' he said kindly. I answered, 'Yeah, everything's OK', and he said, 'Well, thank you... bye', so I left. He has a gorgeous one," she says quietly, "and it's quite clean. I could not believe what had just occurred! I told Lisa, and she jumped up and down, saying, 'That's wonderful! I'm so delighted for you! We got into her SUV and drove around for an hour. I sucked Kid Rock's cock. That was my Mount Everest; out of all of them, he is the most well-known worldwide. His new CD was out yesterday, and I purchased tickets for his April engagement. I have the tenth row. But I'm going to find an empty seat along the railing. I must be in the first four rows on the floor or the first row on the side of the stage. I want them to notice me and make eye contact. If I'm twelve rows back, they won't notice me. Unless I do what I did during the Keith Urban show: rise up in my seat and flash them. But they don't always notice it. You may need to flash them several times before they notice you. I'm spoiled because once you're front row centre, there's no turning back. "That is the Big Kahuna".

Tina had barely touched her grilled cheese and appeared unexpectedly melancholy. "After I've spent time with a band and the show has ended, I get After-Show Depression. When everything is going on, the music and the excitement reach my innermost core. Then they depart, and I feel empty afterwards."

Does she find her real life boring? "My daughter adds so much to my life, but without her, I'd be dragged down by the same old routine of school, work, and internship." When you're in a band, you're sharing something very unique at that moment. You are intimate and close— you receive a piece of them, and they get a bit of your soul."

I pay for the terrible breakfast and go out into the early morning, arm in arm with Tina. "I'm really psyched right now because there are three good concerts coming up in the next couple of months" , she exclaims cheerfully. "Kid Rock, LA Guns, and INXS!" When I first saw JD Fortune, the new INXS vocalist, my heart melted and I felt weak in the knees. He is not just attractive, but magnificent. I've had crushes on rock stars before, but not this bad. I feel like I know him, and the fact that he's vegetarian is quite unusual. Amber recognizes him now and likes his song 'Pretty Vegas'. It's adorable; when I play his video, she says, 'JD! JD!' and points to him, saying, 'Dada'. I answer, "No, that is not Dada, sweetie." JD is much cuter than Dada'".

I'd been back home for a few weeks when Tina sent me an email with animated smiley faces indicating she needed to chat to me. Debbie answers the phone and informs me that Tina is shovelling snow, so I use the chance to inquire about her daughter's groupie adventures. "That's fine with me." "If that's what she wants to do, more power to her," Debbie replies. Debbie then asks quietly, "Did Tina tell you that she gave JD Fortune a blow job?" She certainly did. "She said, 'Come here, JD', then whispered in his ear, 'How would you like a blow job?' and the manager took her on the tour bus."

Miss Tina King had another wish come true.

When I congratulate Tina on her most recent triumph, she is overjoyed. "I never imagined that would happen. Kid Rock is the most famous artist I've worked with, and I didn't expect lightning to strike twice! It was even better because I didn't have a crush on Kid Rock, despite thinking he was attractive. But seeing JD's story each week on TV? "It felt like I knew him already."

Tina found out when INXS will be visiting her local radio station and waited in the foyer. "Then, BOOM, there he was, wearing his 'I Love PETA' T-shirt", she said with delight. "I've met perhaps forty or fifty bands since meeting Whitesnake in 1985. I've never been star struck; I simply call them by their names and treat them as humans. Of course, some people seek to be revered. They desire the enormous brouhaha because it feeds their ego. So I gave JD a huge embrace and lifted him off the ground. He stands 6920 inches tall and weighs approximately 145 pounds. He laughed and responded, 'OK, OK!' Then I laid him down and said, "Please take our picture!" While we were getting our pictures shot, I reached behind and gripped JD's ass. He began giggling and exclaimed, 'Oh my God, she just grabbed my ass!'"

Tina sat near the bus after the "phenomenal" concert. "I was the only one there; I departed after the first encore. I knew I needed to be right there so I could get to him quickly. I yelled, 'JD, JD! I got a flower for you! Everyone was pushing him in different directions, like a ping-pong ball being hurled. As he was ready to board the bus, I said, "JD, hurry!" I've got something to tell you. He approached, leaned in, and I murmured, 'Do you want a blow job?' He smiled broadly and replied, 'Yes!' I was flabbergasted, thinking, 'He's just trying to be polite because he's a lovely man, and I'm sure he gets this question all the time. Okay, be calm. Breathe and count to 10. One minute later, the tour manager grabbed my arm and ushered me onto the bus. It was surreal. I had wanted to give him a blow job since the first time I saw him in episode one, and it was finally happening! I passed by the backing singers and remarked, 'Hey, girls, nice show!' JD was in the far rear of the bus, much like Kid Rock. An attendant was putting down the shades and emptying cigarette buttons before she stepped out and closed the door. JD asked, 'Did you really mean what you said out there?' 'Hell yes, I meant it. Let's do it! He looked like a kid in a candy store, a little nervous. I shoved him down on the couch. He appeared to be thinking, 'She's forceful. I am liking this. Of course, he pulled his pants down, and I began sucking his dick, but it wasn't hard. I was thinking, 'I've given a lot of blow jobs and never received any complaints. Am I becoming rusty? So I told him, 'Honey, it's not becoming hard; you're going to have to help me out here'. He explained, 'Well, darling, I just finished performing for two hours, you know'. I had never heard that if someone provides a really muscular or emotional performance, he may not develop a hard-on. I was thinking, 'I'm just rusty, and he's definitely gotten a lot of fantastic blow jobs. So he helped me out by masturbating while I suck his dick. He then stated, 'This isn't a favorable position for me'. He stood up and turned me around, assertively pulling my pants down and fingering me. I wanted to have sex but didn't ask because I was too frightened. Then he remarked, 'I want to look at your magnificent tits'. I took off my hoodie and was bare-chested. He played with my titties and licked on them before I returned to giving him the blow job. I asked, 'Do you want to give me a facial?' He said, 'Yeah!' So that is what happened. He got all on my face. There was also a lot of come. It was all over my face and chin, except for my eyes. He then exclaimed, 'Oh, that was hot!' When I asked for a towel, he began wiping my face tenderly, delicately, sweetly, and considerately. He stood up, put his clothes back on, and exclaimed, "Oh, damn, that was hot." Your tits are stunning'. I said, 'Thank you', and he said, 'Let me walk you out', and what did I do, like a dumb ass? I've just taken off. I was so terrified out that I didn't say goodbye. I'm very disappointed in myself since I wanted to ask questions that aren't on any of his websites. I wanted to know when and why he became a vegetarian. He's a member of PETA, which I've been with since 1990. But I didn't get to tell him any of this. I wanted to know how it felt to suddenly become highly famous after being homeless and living in his car. I wanted to talk to him like a human being. I wanted to know what makes 'Jason' tick, what moves his heart and soul, but I didn't receive any of it. I understood the sexual aspect, but it left me wanting more. I'm curious what he thinks of me. He probably thinks I'm simply using him, or that I do this all the time. If I had stayed and talked to him, I could have asked, 'Hey, you want to go to a vegetarian restaurant and talk?' INXS is touring Canada for two months, and I'm ready to go. I informed my mother, 'Just so you know, we're heading to Canada. She's not enthusiastic about it. She answered, "Amber and I have to go with you." They are welcome to come, but they will not accompany me to the concert."

Chapter 17: Size Queen of the Stars

S.Static Beth of Boston, Massachusetts, began her voyage to infamy in July 2003, when she was named Sludgette of the Month at www.metal sludge. Fascinated by the penis chart, she began feeding her fixation by compiling naked images of rock musicians displaying their best attributes, which she refers to as a "visual version" of the list. If you want to see Beth's growing collection, go to www.staticbeth.com, click on "Photos", then "Naughty", and browse the list. There are asses ("There's so much ass on this website that the page had to be split in two"), balls and pubes (from Chris Cornell's "Ball Sack" to Slash's pubes), famous cocks, and unsigned cocks. Since my website (www.pamela des barres.com) is one of her connections, I contacted Static Beth to ask a few essential questions and truly enjoyed her sardonic sense of humour.

Pamela: What prompted you to develop this really interesting chart?

Beth: I used to have my own tiny website with Playgirl images. I thought, "I'll just scan the photos and post them up. "It will be cute." It started to catch on. People started emailing me weird naked photographs of celebs, so I purchased my own domain.

Pamela: Do you mind being dubbed a "groupie"?

Beth: I actually have groupie boots in my closet. They haven't come out in a while.

Pamela: How did groupiedom start for you?

Beth: Oh my God, anything for Guns 'N Roses! I send Axl a birthday card every year. I am unwell. I am very unwell. Every time I go to Los Angeles, I drive up his hill. I even stole his newspaper. It was in the driveway, and I thought, "I've got to grab something of his!"

Pamela: Have you had any flings or relationships with rock guys?

Beth: Yes, I do. The majority of my male buddies are in bands. I enjoy the lifestyle. I am a typical girl. Only my employer and a few coworkers know what I do at night. By day, I work for a news agency. Then I hang out with these guys at night. They travel from city to city, appear on television, in films, and throughout the Internet. I try not to be too star-struck. It gives them large heads.

Now it's strange because when they see me, they say, "Ooh, it's Penis Girl!" "Static, Beth!" Either they love me or they flee away. "Oh no, you're the dick girl" .

Pamela: You're famous. How are you feeling about that?

Beth: I'm not sure, but I find it more entertaining than anything else.

Pamela, do you consider yourself a size queen?

Beth: Yes, I do. Although I believe some guys are terrified by it: "If I have a small one, I sure don't want to go with her".

Pamela: Many of the males on your site aren't that big.

Beth: The enormous ones are an exception. Not everyone looks like Tommy Lee. Phil Varone's is long, girthy, and pierced. That bad guy would certainly cut me in two, but I like looking at it. Some of them are very terrible, such as the Marilyn Manson ones. I am like, "Poor boy. "Poor Dita."

Pamela: Well, he isn't hard in the picture.

Beth: I know individuals who have been with him, and it doesn't get any bigger than that.

Pamela: It's unfortunate that there aren't as many renowned groupies these days. I adore your website and how you're carrying on the groupie legacy in such a unique way.

Beth: Appreciate it! With the Internet, everyone knows who has been with whom. It felt better while you were doing your job. Now the guys may share their stories. I'll tell you a little story of mine. I used to hang out with Joey Jordison, the drummer from Slipknot. He's the most well-known artist I've worked with, having won a Grammy Award. It started out nice, but then this other groupie chick came out and said I chatted about him on message boards, which I had never done. She also informed him he was on my website, although he wasn't, and he absolutely turned on me.

Pamela: He apparently enjoys dressing up like a small girl, complete with smeared lipstick and clothing.

Beth: He also enjoys wetting the bed. I'm not sure if she told you that. He's a big bedwetter. He's quite bizarre. He enjoys throwing up on stage. It helps him feel better. He wears a dress and resembles a naked little boy. I call him the Forehead because he has the largest forehead I've ever seen in my life!

Pamela: Do you have any happier groupie stories to share?

Beth: I've got a better one. This is with Racci Shay, who appeared in Dope. I approached him at the show and handed him my business card. He stared at me and said, "Are you Static Beth?" "Oh my God, I was just talking about you!" They were on tour with Mushroomhead, and he and the band's guitarist, Bronson, were gazing at their cocks on my website before the show. He said, "I'm very excited to meet you. He whipped out his cock, lit it on fire, and shouted, "I've been dying to show you this!"

Pamela: Please tell me you have a camera.

Beth: Oh, the photographs are on my website! He said, "Blow out the candle". I blew it out, and we were inseparable for the remainder of the night. He was my biggest fan and was thrilled to be hanging out with me. He introduced me to everyone, "This is Static Beth. "My cock is on her website!"

Pamela: Were most of them already aware about Static Beth?

Beth: They knew. It was funny. Racci stated, "Bronson wants to see you." We were about to board Mushroomhead's bus, but were stopped by their roadie, who shouted, "You can't go on there. Bronson's girlfriend is on the bus, and she dislikes the photographs on your website." I thought, "I've been cock-blocked!" I couldn't get on Mushroomhead's bus. It's unfortunate since she should be proud of him! Anyway, Racci and I were drinking and he asked, "Do you want to go to the bathroom? "I have to pee." So I went with him, and he asked, "Will you hold it?" I positioned his cock at him so he could pee in the urinal, and he exclaimed, "Hey, you're pretty good". Later on, we were hanging out and doing typical silly band photos. Racci suddenly took down my shirt in the middle of the venue, with everyone standing about, and began licking my boobs. He then asked if I wanted to go to the back room, and I answered, 'OK'. He demonstrated the trick with the match again and asked, "Do you want to blow me?" I replied, "Why not?" So we entered the boiler room. It was dusty, stinky, and unpleasant. So I went down and did my thing, and in the midst of it, he asked, "Do you want to fuck?" Very casual, as in "Do you want a piece of gum?" And I replied, "All right. "Do you have a condom?" he asked, and he responded, "Oh, yeah. I'm a Boy Scout," and I said, "Excellent!" We were having sex in the boiler room, and the floor was built of brick. He suddenly started laughing. I asked, "What?" He replied, "My foot is trapped in the brickwork! Give me one second," and he eventually untangled his foot. I grabbed something, and my palm was completely covered in soot. When it was all over, we came out fully covered in dirt. It was really funny. And how odd. The entire night was really unpredictable.

Pamela: Would he have been your first pick for the band?

Beth: Because he performed that flame thing on his penis. I thought, "I love this guy. "He is so cute." It was a very enjoyable experience. I hadn't expected anything. Sometimes I think, "Oh, I really like you," but it was nothing like that. It was simply, "OK, we're done". He took his drink and left, and I went home delighted.

Pamela: So, like many groupies, do your feelings become twisted up?

Beth: Oh, yes. I've been hurt several times. So it was a positive experience for me because there were no strings connected. Actually, I think it was exciting for him. He was with Static. Beth.

Pamela: He was your groupie.

Beth: He was! He was my tiny fan. Pamela: Have you been likened to Cindy Plaster Caster?

Beth: Yes. I love her website. I am sure you have seen it, with the sperm squirting.

Pamela: That's wonderful. I believe you are also providing a service through your website. People are so tense, and what you're doing is refreshing. You're reminding folks that it's just a dick, for goodness sake!

Beth: There is no other site like it, unless you want to see gay porn. There isn't much out there for women who enjoy the music scene.

Pamela: And it's clear that the rock guys enjoy being shown on your website. That's why it's so effective!

Made in the USA
Monee, IL
17 February 2025

12493086R00079